This book is dedicated to every angel in heaven for the guidance, comfort, and protection they offer us here on earth each day, with special gratitude to the angels who constantly sent me messages and inspiration during the writing process.

I would like to thank Linda Konner, Angela Wix, my husband, all my family on both the Carroll and Richardson sides, my in-laws, my friends, my dad, my brother, Amy, Cathryn, Paulette, Rae, Keith Moon, and my mother, Jana.

ANGEL
INSIGHTS

Photo by Devin Cruz

About the Author

Tanya Carroll Richardson is the author of *Heaven on Earth: A Guided Journal for Creating Your Own Divine Paradise* (Sterling Ethos). *Angel Insights* marks her first book with Llewellyn.

To Write to the Author

If you wish to contact the author or would like more information about this book, please write to the author in care of Llewellyn Worldwide, and we will forward your request. Both the author and publisher appreciate hearing from you and learning of your enjoyment of this book and how it has helped you. Llewellyn Worldwide cannot guarantee that every letter written to the author can be answered, but all will be forwarded. Please write to:

Tanya Carroll Richardson
℅ Llewellyn Worldwide
2143 Wooddale Drive
Woodbury, MN 55125-2989

Please enclose a self-addressed stamped envelope for reply,
or $1.00 to cover costs. If outside the USA, enclose
an international postal reply coupon.

TANYA CARROLL RICHARDSON

ANGEL INSIGHTS

Inspiring Messages from
and Ways to Connect with
Your Spiritual Guardians

Llewellyn Worldwide
Woodbury, Minnesota

FIRST EDITION
First Printing, 2016

Book design by Bob Gaul
Cover images by iStockphoto.com/11910139/©DrPAS
iStockphoto.com/68765419/©Ben Harding
Shutterstock/128088929/©Ase
Shutterstock/287082455/©groodday28
Cover design by Kevin R. Brown
Editing by Rhiannon Nelson

Llewellyn Publications is a registered trademark of Llewellyn Worldwide Ltd.

Library of Congress Cataloging-in-Publication Data
Names: Richardson, Tanya Carroll, 1974– author.
Title: Angel insights : inspiring messages from and ways to connect with your
   spiritual guardians / Tanya Carroll Richardson.
Description: First Edition. | Woodbury : Llewellyn Worldwide, Ltd, 2016. |
   Includes bibliographical references.
Identifiers: LCCN 2015048795 (print) | LCCN 2015049895 (ebook) | ISBN
   9780738747958 | ISBN 9780738749037 ()
Subjects: LCSH: Angels.
Classification: LCC BL477 .R53 2016 (print) | LCC BL477 (ebook) | DDC
   202/.15—dc23
LC record available at http://lccn.loc.gov/2015048795

Llewellyn Worldwide Ltd. does not participate in, endorse, or have authority or responsibility with private business transactions between authors and the public.

All mail addressed to the author is forwarded, but the publisher cannot, unless specifically instructed by the author, give out an address or phone number.

Any Internet references contained in this work are current at publication time, but the publisher cannot guarantee that a specific location will continue to be maintained. Please refer to the publisher's website for links to authors' websites and other sources.

Llewellyn Publications
A Division of Llewellyn Worldwide Ltd.
2143 Wooddale Drive
Woodbury, MN 55125-2989
www.llewellyn.com

Printed in the United States of America

Contents

Introduction

Do you ever wish you could get a clear message from your guardian angels? Ask them for advice when you are feeling down, celebrate with them when you're on top of the world, gain wisdom about life and Spirit from your angels?

Maybe the idea of angels has always resonated with you, but you don't really know much about them. Or maybe you occasionally sense that you're getting a message from an angel, but you want to feel a stronger bond to the angel realm and wish to communicate with angels frequently. Whether you want to learn more about angels, want to learn how to receive guidance from your angels, or are an old hand at angelic communication and just want to pick up some new tricks, this book will help you create a closer connection to the angel realm.

Everyone has guardian angels. They were assigned to you at birth, and they are devoted to protecting you and advocating for you throughout your life. Your guardian angels are a gift from Spirit, but they are a gift you do not have to earn—a gift that will never be taken back. The love and healing energy of your guardian angels is your birthright. This book discusses several different types of angels, but will often reference guardian angels, as those are the angels you will have the most intimate relationships with throughout your life. However, this book can help you create a closer connection to not only your guardian angels but the angel realm as a whole.

In this book you will learn more about guardian angels—who they are, what their commitment is to you, what they can do for you, and what they can't do for you. You will have many angels come and go throughout your life, showing up to help you navigate certain situations, offering healing from physical pain or emotional trauma, or teaching you specific knowledge as it becomes needed during your life journey. But your guardian angels are your core angels, and they are with you, every moment, through thick and thin. Their love and devotion to you is like that of Spirit—it knows no bounds. In addition to guardian angels, we'll examine archangels and helper angels and the roles they can play in your life.

This book also offers the angel realm's perspective on spiritual topics such as fate, free will, divine timing, and soul contracts. These messages from the angel realm will help reveal the enormous part Spirit plays in our earthly journey, as well as the practical details of Spirit's influence. Many of these angel messages will help explain how angels work in our lives, and what angels want us to personally work on and work toward. I hope you find these angel messages enlightening, thought-provoking, inspiring, and comforting.

Throughout the book you'll be given many angel exercises to help you strengthen your bond with the angel realm. These exercises should increase your ability to recognize and receive angelic guidance. They will encourage you to seek the help, healing, and counsel of your angels more often. Many of the exercises are designed to bring you closer to the angel realm by inspiring you to see the world through the eyes of an angel, increasing your sense of compassion and tenderness, and encouraging you to act as a human angel in the world.

Each chapter contains several angel affirmations and angel prayers. These tools give you a quick, easy way to call upon the angels, or align yourself with the angel realm. Work with these prayers and affirmations anytime, anyplace. If a section in one of the chapters particularly resonates with you, or you find that section challenging, definitely spend some time working with the affirmation or prayer from that section. Affirmations help recalibrate our subconscious mind, which affects the energy we give off, what we attract into our lives, and how we feel about ourselves. Prayer enables us to call upon the angel realm for guidance and intercession.

I recommend keeping a journal, if you don't already, while you read this book. Journaling is a wonderful way to express your feelings, set goals for the future, understand your past, and generally get to know yourself better. But it's also a fantastic way to get closer to Spirit and the angel realm. There are several exercises in this book that require a journal. Keep in mind that you don't have to spend a lot of money on your journal: It can be a plain, cheap one you pick up at the drugstore—although having a pretty journal is helpful, as that will make you want to pick it up more often. You can either spend a few extra dollars on a journal with a pretty cover, or decorate a plain journal by drawing on the cover or pasting pictures on it. For more about journaling, see chapter six.

I've been working with angels for more than ten years—coming to them for guidance, emotional healing, grace, insight, and assistance. Some of the information in this book was intuitively given to me by my own guardian angels, helper angels, and archangels who were by my side as I faithfully typed away on my computer keyboard. This information was communicated to me through clairaudience, clairvoyance, clairsentience, and claircognizance. Clairvoyance, or being given information intuitively through pictures, is a skill that I only began utilizing a few years ago. I am naturally very clairaudient, which means I hear intuitive guidance, and I was thrilled when I began receiving pictures as guidance from the angel realm. I knew it meant my work on trusting and honing my intuition was paying off, and being able to receive pictures as guidance from the angels assisted me immensely in writing this book. Honing and trusting your own intuition will also pay off for you in the form of increased guidance from the angels. The angel exercises in this book will help you get in touch with and hone your own intuition.

I interact with angels—guardian angels, helper angels, and archangels—closely and directly on a daily basis. This is, and has been for some time, "normal" for me. Yet I have never felt the presence of the angel realm as strongly as when I was writing this book, and I have to thank the angels for giving me such precious insight to share with you. Over the past decade I've written about angels regularly and talked to hundreds of people about their encounters with angels. I've had folks share their stories with me about angels offering them healing, angels offering them guidance, angels giving them peace or encouragement, and angels saving their lives. Learning about angels is obviously a passion of mine—I devour books and videos that offer information on the angel realm and am always on the lookout for new insights. I also offer private Angel Readings, and have learned much about how angels operate by intuitively reading individuals of all walks of life.

Angels are constantly trying to reach us—through our thoughts, our feelings, children, animals, nature, music, and the synchronicities that show up in our lives. Communicating with angels is possible for everyone, but it does take some practice for most people. For you it may be just a matter of meditating about your angels or journaling to them. Or it might take a little more time and effort. In either case, I encourage you to get to know your angels personally. In the meantime, if you are struggling with a certain emotion, trying to make sense of a common situation, or longing for wisdom about your role here on earth as a spiritual being in a physical body, the angel messages in this book contain reassuring guidance from angels that applies to anyone's life.

You can read the book in chronological order, look though the table of contents to find a topic that appeals to you, or (and this is my personal favorite) open the book up at random to see what message, exercise, or information your own guardian angels want you to utilize. (Your guardian angels will lead you to the page that will resonate deepest with you, or teach you what you most need to know in the present moment.)

Angels want to play a bigger role in your life, and they want you to feel closer to them. Your guardian angels in particular are always available to you and eager to strengthen your bond with them and increase back-and-forth communication. Angels are more like humans than you realize—they have hearts and souls, and they can understand your joys and your sorrows. As you read the angel messages in this book, learn more about who angels are, practice the angel exercises, and work with the angel prayers and affirmations that accompany each angel message, know that your own guardian angels are reading right along with you.

1

---●---

Who Are Angels?

First, I want to share with you how excited the angels are about this book. Angels love books about angels! As I've been working on this book, the angels have sent me strong messages and made their presence often known. Your own guardian angels are thrilled that you picked up this book. They know it means you want to have a closer relationship with them and learn how to better communicate with angels in general.

There is an angel for every time and purpose under heaven. Angels who watch over you from birth until you return to Spirit, angels who help you heal, angels who are teachers, even angels who can assist you in marketing a product! We'll learn about many of them in this section. But remember, there are always angels uniquely qualified to help you with even the most specific, esoteric tasks. The angel realm is asking me to assure you that there are angels equipped for the digital age, who can aid you with modern problems or anything new you are trying to invent. The angels tell me they are "light-years" ahead of us regarding these matters. All you have to do is request their help.

Guardian Angels

Let's start by discussing the type of angel people are most familiar with: guardian angels. Your guardian angels are different from your helper angels, and your guardian angels are not archangels. You will have relationships with many angels throughout your life, but the relationship you have with your guardian angels is the most intimate, the most constant.

Angels are Spirit's helpers, Spirit's right-hand entities. Think of Spirit as a conductor, and angels are musicians in a divine orchestra. Every musician has a unique part to play, and the part of each guardian angel is crucial, enormous: to guide and protect a single human life.

Your guardian angels were assigned to you at birth and took sacred vows to protect you and advocate for you throughout your soul's journey on this planet. The energy of your guardian angels is a maternal energy: devoted, unconditional, protective. I'm not talking about a human maternal energy, but an archetypal one. A maternal energy that is divine and what we would think of as "perfect" or "ideal" or "pure."

Have you ever had a child enter your life? Perhaps your own child or the child of a family member or close friend. Do you recall how it felt to hold that infant in your arms? To notice how small and delicate it was? To sense the sacred charge that comes with realizing how much this precious little being needs your affection, guidance, and protection? That is how your guardian angels feel about you. Not just when you were a baby, but when you are an adult in your prime, as you mature into the final days of your life, and every stage in between. Your guardian angels' sense of duty toward you is not a job, but a calling. Like a mother, their calling is a labor of love.

Angels are noble creatures, creatures of virtue and honor. And your guardian angels have sworn loyalty to you. It is a promise made with great ceremony and soberness. A promise made to you and to Spirit, witnessed by every other angel in heaven.

Each human has guardian angels. And yes, I believe that is *angels*, plural. How many guardian angels you have varies from person to person, and I suspect the amount has something to do with the life path and challenges each individual soul will experience on earth. I was told by the angel realm that I have nine guardian angels. My initial thought was, *So many, just for me?* The answer I heard immediately back from the angel realm was, "You deserve it." And you know what? We each deserve all of our guardian angels. Your guardian angels are a gift from Spirit. But they are a gift you do not have to earn, a gift that will never be taken back. The love and healing energy of your guardian angels is your birthright.

Your guardian angels will never abandon you, never forsake you, never punish you, never judge you. This knowledge can be very comforting for those who were abandoned or abused either as a child or an adult, and for these people I believe it is especially healing to develop greater communication with, and a closer bond to, their guardian angels.

Your guardian angels already know the flight plan of your life, as it was laid out before your birth, just like your soul is already aware of many of the sorrows, challenges, accomplishments, and joys you will experience here on earth. Your guardian angels have agreed to stay with you during all of these predestined events as well as see you through the wild-card aspects of your life, which are undecided and in constant flux. Your guardian angels will help you face any foe, walk through any fear, and savor all the joy and pleasure in life. They will never leave you, no matter how grave the danger, just as they will never decide that your life is going so well that you simply don't need them anymore. They are in it for better or worse.

You are the top priority of your guardian angels. They are always with you. They never have something more important or more pressing to be concerned with. Like a mother forever trailing behind her curious, active toddler to make sure the child stays out of trouble, so your guardian angels are always hovering nearby. Your guardian angels are so closely linked to you that they will often know your needs and desires before you do, just as a mother knows the signs that show a child is hungry or tired. This is how angels can save people from accidents in a split second, or bring you an unexpected treat or change to your schedule that leaves you thinking, *Wow, I didn't realize it until now, but this was exactly what I needed today.*

Although your guardian angels are creatures that possess phenomenal power and gifts, there is a limit to how much they can help you. If it is someone's time to pass on to heaven, a guardian angel cannot interfere and save their life. Nor can a guardian angel save you from an experience that your soul chose to be a part of (illness, war, etc.), either to help someone else, heal the planet, or simply to learn and grow. Your guardian angels are also bound by your own free will. They can give you guidance and send people and resources into your life to aid you, but it is often up to you to accept or deny this help, to act on this guidance or not.

What *can* your guardian angels do? They can help you achieve the divine missions your soul came to earth to accomplish. They perform this feat by giving you intuitive information about the best decisions you can make in a situation, decisions that lead to your highest good, the highest good of those around you, and your best possible life. They help you by sending advantageous people and opportunities to you. And they help you by comforting you, and giving you their strength and courage. Your guardian angels will always guide and protect you, but because you have free will the more you invite your angels to assist you, the greater role they can play in your life.

The main reason your guardian angels are so excited to see you reading this book is because they want to have a closer connection with you. Your guardian angels know the more you learn about them, and the better you get at communicating with them, the more you will ask for your guardian angels' assistance, the more you will recognize their presence, and the more your guardian angels can guide you and aid you.

Angel Affirmation: My guardian angels always have my back. Because of my guardian angels, I know I will never walk alone.

Angel Exercise:
Learn the Names of Your Guardian Angels

Feel closer to your guardian angels by calling them by name. For this exercise, go to a room that is quiet, where you can shut the door to block out other people's energy and concentrate. Sit still, close your eyes, calm your mind, and ask your higher self for the name of one of your guardian angels. Often your higher self or one of your guardian angels will answer by placing the name into your head. This name might appear as written letters in your mind: S-A-R-A, for example. Or you might hear the name *Sara* whispered into your ear. This exercise can be repeated as often as you like, until you feel you have received the names of all of your guardian angels. Some angels have regal names, like Celestia, while other names might be more practical, like the name of one of *my* guardian angels, Sharon. Once you ask, the first name that pops into your head is the most accurate.

Don't despair if you try this exercise for a few minutes and no name comes. Take a break and try the exercise again later on. If you feel like you can't get a solid intuitive hit on a name, it might be that your guardian angels are inviting *you* to give them names.

If this is the case, give each of your guardian angels a name that makes you feel cherished and protected every time you think of it. When I was told by the angel realm that one of my guardian angels is named Samantha, I had to laugh. It was my favorite name as a little girl, which is why I named my beloved teddy bear Samantha, a teddy bear I kept with me even through college, long after I had outgrown stuffed animals. Obviously I loved that name because my guardian angel was whispering her name in my ear, and obviously I loved that teddy bear so much because it was, unbeknownst to my conscious mind, a connection to my angels. If there is a name you have always been attracted to, it might be the name of one of your guardian angels.

Come up with two or three names, and then ask if there are still more guardian angels assigned to you who would like nicknames. You'll know you've come up with a good guardian angel nickname if thinking of it or saying it out loud makes you feel warm and peaceful, gives you chills and the hairs on your arms stand up, or brings a smile to your face. You can use this exercise for every member of your family, because every person has guardian angels assigned to them at birth.

Write down the names of your guardian angels, and feel free to call them by name when you ask them for comfort or guidance. In time you may get to know each of your guardian angels better, even sensing their individual personalities, learning which guardian angel is best to call upon in different situations, etc. My guardian angel Sharon has a very comforting, nurturing personality. Another guardian angel of mine named Grace is very optimistic and reverent. And Lucinda is a guardian angel assigned to me who is dramatic and a bit of a diva (she's great to call upon when I need to bring out my own inner diva).

Using your guardian angels' names might help you stay more connected to them, or make your guardian angels seem more "real" to you. Asking for help or guidance for a family member by addressing your loved one's guardian angels by name can also make you feel more empowered and connected to the angel realm.

Helper Angels

Besides guardian angels, each human also has access to an endless amount of helper angels. Unlike guardian angels who stay with you throughout your life, helper angels usually come and go. They appear when a need arises, and then fly away when their job is finished.

Like archangels, helper angels each have certain areas of expertise. If you are working on launching a new product, you might pray for some PR helper angels to lend a wing with your publicity campaign. PR helper angels might send you great marketing ideas and perfect people to pitch for press coverage. If you are facing an intimidating diagnosis, ask for healing helper angels to surround you with their transformational energy. Healing helper angels can also gift you and your healthcare providers with the wisdom required for your recovery, and give you the courage and peace to face the healing or chronic-illness management journey ahead.

There are countless angels in heaven to aid you, and there are specific helper angels qualified to handle any request you offer up. Some helper angels might only be with you for an afternoon; if, for example, you ask for a helper angel who specializes in fashion and shopping to assist you in picking out the ideal dress. Other helper angels could be with you for decades if the project requires it. For example, you may be a concert pianist who asks for a helper angel who specializes in music and performance. This angel might remain with you throughout your career.

The angels told me that you can get as specific as you want when requesting a helper angel. If you are a singer, one helper angel might be a voice coach, another angel can help you with stage presence, another angel could help you with stage clothes, another angel would help you in choosing songs and arrangements, and still another angel might help with management and bookings. Get the idea?

Helper angels are not often committed to being at your side throughout your entire life, as guardian angels are, but helper angels are still devoted, loving creatures. Some of your helper angels may have even been assigned to you before birth, when your life path was being designed by Spirit. Those helper angels probably agreed to be with you during important transitions, and see you through pivotal projects and relationships at set times in your life. These helper angels will show up whether you ask them to or not. Other helper angels needed for less serious, critical issues might only appear if you let them know you want their input.

Helper angels are highly capable experts in their fields. They are professional and possess abilities that can really bring the wow factor to any project or situation. After all, no one has higher standards than heaven! Each helper angel will aid you the same way any other angel would: by sending you enlightened ideas, appropriate partners, unique opportunities, and, of course, straight-up miracles.

Angel Affirmation: Helper angels possess a diverse array of skills and specialties, and are always available to assist me with any task. All I have to do is ask!

If You See an Angel...

Fear not. This is the Bible's suggestion when you see an angel, and it's great advice. But why *would* you be afraid if, for instance, your guardian angel—someone who loves you unconditionally and eternally—appeared before you? After writing about angels for more than a decade, I've had many people share with me their encounters with these beings of light, and I've read about still more, both modern encounters with angels and ancient tales of humans communing with these magnificent, diverse, and dynamic divine creatures. Usually people sense an angel's presence, or hear an angel's voice, but sometimes folks actually see an angel.

Humans who see these entities are sometimes, though certainly not always, *initially* terrified at being in the presence of a divine angel with wings. Many times these are folks who believe in angels, and know that angels are benevolent creatures devoted to serving, loving, and protecting humans. Therefore I never understood why seeing an angel would provoke a sense of fear in humans...until I saw an angel myself.

One day I was in my bedroom at home working on a project, so engrossed that I hadn't looked away from the computer screen for some time. Suddenly I sensed a presence behind me. I could feel their energy, and the skin on my neck tingled like a kind of primal alarm system. I glanced up to see if someone, maybe my husband, had entered the room. Over my writing desk, which faced a wall, hung a large mirror. When I looked up at the mirror I could always see who was walking in the bedroom door behind me. But when I looked into the mirror that day I gasped. Standing just behind my desk chair was an angel: tall and graceful and very real. Although she appeared muted and soft, I could make out her features and her dress very clearly. She appeared to me the way most people report seeing a divine angel in physical form: wearing a long white robe with hair that fell in ringlets around her shoulders, donning a golden rope at her waist, and possessing two gigantic wings covered in hundreds of white feathers. The sheer size of these wings alone terrified me! Her wings seemed so powerful. In fact, there was an energy coming off this incredible being that was, frankly, intimidating. I knew at once when I saw her that this was a mighty creature, capable of more than I could guess.

My heart beat hard and fast in my chest while the rest of me sat there still as a deer surprised in the woods, watching this otherworldly being in the mirror as she slowly moved—floated—out of view. The whole experience lasted about thirty seconds. Once I felt able I turned around in my chair. The room was empty—or at least it appeared to my human eyes that the room was now empty.

The angel I saw was exactly as many others have described. Of course I have heard different versions of this image over the years (please also note that people I've spoken with have seen angels—with wings—of all ethnicities). I learned later from the angels that the angel I saw is named Samantha, and she is one of my lead guardian angels. Samantha brings me wisdom and insight from the angel realm and the world of Spirit in general. That's a big role to play in my life and I am indebted to this angel for her constant assistance. And it explains her presence in my bedroom that day: I was working on my guided journal, *Heaven on Earth*. Samantha had obviously come to guide me as I wrote. Now I know that even though I can't always see her, this guardian angel is always right beside me when I am working on a book.

Later, of course, like many people who are initially frightened by encountering a divine angel in physical form, seeing an angel became one of my most treasured memories. But at the moment my angel sighting was happening, having a being from another dimension with feather wings suddenly appear before me unannounced was incredibly unnerving. For most people, seeing an angel is a once-in-a-lifetime experience. But there are exceptions. There are people, such as Irish author and activist Lorna Byrne, who see angels often. Some people are good at math, and some people are good at seeing angels! And although I hear angels often, I don't normally see them. No matter what society, or any individual, would have you believe, in spiritual truth none of us is more worthy or special than another. We each have unique talents and gifts. When I have asked the angel realm about Lorna Byrne, the word that comes to me is *witness*. She was singled out to bear unique witness to the angel realm by seeing angels often, and to share what she experiences with the world, just as each of us is given certain experiences and opportunities to share something unique and important with the world—whether that is directly touching the lives of a few people or millions. (When I asked the angels about me, the word they gave me was *messenger*. I do believe I am destined to recieve messages from Spirit and share them with others.) Remember, even if you are not influencing on the scale that an author like Lorna is, everyone you touch, aid, heal, love, protect, or teach has an impact on many other lives. The angels are showing me an image of a single drop of water hitting a pond. There is a ripple effect to all your actions, just like the drop of water has a ripple effect, and just as its presence contributes to the size and makeup of the pond as a whole. Lorna is very precious, but so are you. And whether you see angels or not, they are always nearby, and the angels are asking me to tell you that they love each and every one of us "enormously."

Other common ways angels appear—in distilled divine states similar to having wings—are as a bright or glowing white light, as small dots of colored lights, or as what looks like white vapor or mist. When angels appear in their divine state, they don't tend to say much—or if they do the message is very brief and to the point.

But often angels will take on a human form when they visit you, like when the angel Clarence Odbody visits George Bailey in *It's a Wonderful Life*. It is more typical to see an angel in human form than in their full divine glory (feather wings and flowing robe, or bright white light). Possibly this human disguise is assumed so that the angels won't scare us so badly that we wet our pants when they appear! Can you imagine if George Bailey had been visited by an angel who was not disguised as a human? Considering the day George was having, that might have sent him completely over the edge. Also, assuming a human form allows angels to move freely in public, and interact with *you* in public, if the situation requires this.

I've heard and read far more stories from people who have encountered angels in human form. These angels offer information, comfort, or assistance, and then vanish. The people who interacted with the angel in human form will usually go back to the hospital or police station or store where they saw this helpful person and ask to speak to the individual who assisted them so they can thank them properly. "Never had anyone working here by that name and description" is a standard response. It is only then that these folks realize that the person who saved their life, inspired them, or made them smile was really an angel. Yet when people reflect on the details of their experience with an angel in human form, they probably remember there being something different about this stranger they encountered, something different that was noticeable from the beginning. Angels assuming human form often have very kind eyes, for example, or have a calming, soothing energy that becomes infectious to those around them. They might seem to know everything about you, even though they are strangers. Angels who assume human form are often remarkably sweet tempered and say just the right thing. Or they might appear out of the blue just when help is required, and then vanish just as quickly afterward—without leaving footprints or tire tracks behind them.

No matter how an angel appears to you—in human form or in a divine state—angels tend to manifest in physical form to us at pivotal moments. Angels can materialize in life-and-death situations when you need assistance (an angel might save you from drowning or dying in a car wreck—sometimes in these cases you will not see the angel, only feel their hands pulling you to safety). Angels might show up at a crossroads in your career (an angel in human form might give you wise counsel and encourage you to pursue a certain path, or an angel with wings might appear as you are typing away on a book, signaling you have a potential career as an author). Angels may come around when you desperately need to know you are loved (an angel in human form might visit you like Clarence visited George Bailey and convince you that you are precious and important). Angels may offer their services when you require comfort or courage (an angel in human form might pray with you or hold your hand in a hospital waiting room).

Angels can appear in physical form at small moments too. Angels love to inspire you and aid you even with everyday matters. It's fun for them to show up, assume a human form, and lend a hand when you are stressed or tired or in a jam. That's why you will occasionally encounter an endearing stranger who seems unrealistically happy to change your tire or pick up your tab— it's an angel getting joy from doing a good deed. If a stranger appears right when you need them, and is extremely kind and generous, it could very well be an angel in disguise. If you realize later that it was an angel who helped you, the treasured memory can increase your faith and your connection to the angel realm.

If you have never seen an angel, that does not mean angels aren't with you. You have probably unknowingly encountered an angel in human form. People who have seen an angel in their divine state are not loved more or favored more by Spirit. There simply exists a veil between this world and the next that must remain intact to a degree. I believe when you see an angel in a divine state (wings, bright light) that veil is parted for a moment, and it's an event that just doesn't happen every day and isn't supposed to happen every day to the majority of people. (As always, there are exceptions: People who regularly see spirits or angels.) You may even long to see an angel in its divine state, and pray to see one, and still never have the experience in this life. Why? It's a mystery.

However, making contact with your angels via the other methods discussed in this book (see chapters three, four, and five) is much easier and more common, and can allow you to create daily contact with your angels.

Angel Affirmation: When I hear a story about someone seeing an angel, my guardian angels simply want me to take it as a reminder that they are real and always with me.

Hospitals Are Staffed by Angels

There is a sub-group of helper angels known as hospital angels. Like other healing helper angels, hospital angels' sole purpose is to facilitate healing on an emotional, physical, and spiritual level. But hospital angels aren't assigned to one patient for the duration of their healing journey, as other healing helper angels might be. Nor do hospital angels follow the practice of a single healthcare professional by shadowing him or her exclusively during their work, as healing helper angels will. Hospital angels are just what their name implies: angels who are attached to one hospital as a whole. Hospital angels' allegiance is to everyone in the hospital, just so long as those people are within its walls. An exception would be ambulances or helicopters that transport patients to the hospital. Although not technically located in the hospital, hospital angels are most definitely along for those rides!

Like nurses, technicians, housekeeping staff, and doctors, hospital angels are on call twenty-four hours a day, working in shifts, just as humans work at hospitals in shifts. These angels aren't only hanging out in the hospital chapel (although there is an angel always on duty in the chapel, an angel whose large presence is like a very soft white light, an angel who is an expert at comforting and consoling and restoring hope). Hospital angels are highly skilled celestial candy stripers who roam the halls looking for patients or healthcare professionals in need of assistance. And of course these hospital angels perform daily rounds just like doctors and nurses, where they check up on all the patients in the building.

Whenever you are visiting a healthcare professional in their non-hospital office or small clinic, or are receiving a healing service of any kind, please know there is a healing helper angel present. Wherever there is healing, there are angels. But it can be very reassuring for people who are entering a hospital as a patient, people who are visiting a loved one in the hospital, or folks who work at a hospital to know that they are surrounded by angels specifically assigned to that hospital. Hospitals can be chaotic places where decisions sometimes have to be made very quickly, where life-and-death procedures are performed daily, and where diagnoses that are serious and may come as a shock to the patient and their families are routine. Therefore hospitals can be especially anxiety producing to the people inside. Knowing that Spirit's invisible guardians are all around can do a lot to put those staying, visiting, or working in a hospital at ease.

If you or a loved one is a patient, angels will be doing a lot of hand-holding, working on giving you and your loved one patience, strength, courage, hope, and peace. Likewise these angels will also aid patients on a physical level to help speed up the healing process. Please remember, though, angels cannot save someone if it is their time to pass on. Likewise, an angel cannot spare someone from an injury or an illness that will serve their soul's growth, or enable them to serve others, and is part of a larger divine plan. But angels can do an enormous amount to ensure a patient passes away as peacefully as possible, and they do their best to make sure that patients receive excellent care and plenty of mercy. Don't be surprised if an angel appears to you in human form and is very helpful or consoling. When you ask the hospital staff about this person later, you may get this response: "No one by that name or description works here."

If you are a healthcare professional, it can be daunting to know how much patients depend upon you. Rest assured that there are angels right beside you while you work, providing medical insight, steadying your own emotions, and guiding your hands. You are not alone—you are divinely supported. Hospital angels are exceptional healers, and can help on a very practical level. Picture them in white coats and stethoscopes or in scrubs with masks over their faces—only they are also sporting a giant pair of wings!

The next time you find yourself in a hospital, take a moment to picture angels all around—sitting at the reception desk, standing behind the equipment, sticking to your doctor's side—and breathe a sigh of relief. When you are in the hospital as a patient, visitor, or healthcare professional, you are under the care, guidance, and protection of angels.

Angel Affirmation: There are angels dedicated to serving those who work and heal in hospitals. Whenever I am in a hospital, I am always under an angel's care.

What Are Spirit Guides?

When we talk about receiving messages from Spirit, in truth you could receive spiritual guidance from many different avenues: from angels, from spirit guides, from loved ones who have passed on, from ascended masters, or from Spirit itself—to name a few.

I thought it might be helpful to touch on this briefly, just so you know that not every intuitive insight you get comes from an angel (insights could even come from your own soul, your own higher self). As you work more with the realm of Spirit, you will be able to tell who is talking to you or sending you guidance. There can be a lot of voices running around in your head if you are very intuitive and adept at communicating with the Spirit world. I have gotten to the point in recent years where I can tell if I'm getting a message from my mother who passed away, Jesus, one of my guardian angels (hey, Sharon!), or Spirit itself. In time it is possible that you too can become this in tune with your spiritual support system if you are highly intuitive and work on building your intuitive muscles and connecting with and identifying your spiritual guidance team.

We've already talked about some of the angels you will get messages from: helper angels, archangels, and guardian angels. Again, you can hone in with practice and time and learn to distinguish one angel from another, although it's not necessary to do so. The important thing is the message, not which angel is giving it. I realize I am partial to angels, but I feel most of the intuitive guidance I get comes from angels. This actually makes sense as angels are the messengers of Spirit. Taking our messages up to Spirit and bringing messages back down from heaven is simply one of the things angels do best. Also our guardian angels are devoted to us in a way that other spirits may not be. You should feel comfortable calling on ascended masters such as Jesus and Buddha; you can actually access their energy any time and their spirits are able to be all places at once. But as you know, guiding you is not their entire purpose. However, your guardian angels are always nearby and you are their top priority. Also I don't think spirit guides can jump in and intervene in the dramatic ways an angel can (like saving you from a fire, performing a miracle healing, etc.).

Just like with angels, your spirit guides will deliver guidance, comfort, and inspiration. Spirit guides are usually people who have lived before, are passed on, and have chosen to help you navigate your earthly journey. They will have something important in common with you (mastered a career you are entering, for example). Spirit guides either signed on as your spirit guide via a soul contract before you were born or you picked them up along the way once you got to earth. I'll give two examples of spirit guides of my own, a Native American shaman and Keith Moon, the famous drummer of The Who.

I believe the Native American spirit guide signed on with me before I was born, and perhaps we shared a past life together. I do have Native American heritage (my great-great-grandmother was full-blooded Cherokee) and I have always had an interest in Native American culture. I believe this spirit guide helps connect me to the earth and grounds me in a love of and respect for nature. This spirit guide is also a mystic and can teach me much about connecting to the world of Spirit and the healing arts. I feel this spirit guide's presence with me when I am in nature and sense the holy quality of the earth around me. This spirit guide was also once a warrior as a young man, and I feel him with me whenever I have to find my courage and tackle a big challenge or fight for what I believe in. I imagine that this spirit guide will be with me for life.

Keith and I made a connection after I read a biography of him. I was drawn to his sweet, mischievous energy. I sensed he was very tenderhearted, and that in life he'd had a lot of demons and regrets. I felt he was a highly intelligent, extremely talented romantic who loved deeply, and he communicated to me that his biggest regret was dying young and subsequently not being a part of his daughter's life. Learning about Keith's life and personality helped me understand an important relationship in my own life that was causing me some anxiety at the time (the fact that I love rock and roll—and Keith's drumming—probably helped my bond with Keith too). For a few years, whenever I got upset or down, Keith's favorite song, the Beach Boys' "Don't Worry Baby," would suddenly come on the radio. I don't sense Keith's energy with me very often anymore, because he taught me what I needed to learn from him. (As soon as I finished writing this paragraph about Keith, I went on Facebook and guess what was at the top of my news feed? A live concert video posted by Keith Moon's Facebook page.)

Keep in mind that these spirit guides will still have many of the same personality traits they had in life. If you call upon a famous artist who was a workaholic in life to help you with a project, for example, he might encourage you to burn the midnight oil—perhaps a bit more than you are comfortable with or is good for you.

As you can probably guess, I am only touching on the world of spirit guides and the larger spiritual support system that I believe we each have (again, relatives who have passed on are also part of this support system, and you may feel the presence of a particular loved one on a regular basis, as I do my mother, who I believe has signed on to be one of my spirit guides).

Angel Affirmation: Angels have lots of help in guiding and supporting me. There is a whole team of spirits in heaven who care for me.

Angels of Mercy

If you are scared or hopeless or in pain, one of the most calming, comforting prayers you can offer up is to an angel of mercy. Just calling upon these powerful helper angels will instantly make you feel more peaceful, protected, and hopeful, no matter how intimidating the challenges you face.

Every angel is capable of sprinkling mercy and grace over a situation or person, but there exists a specific group of helper angels who are dedicated to missions of mercy. Angels cannot always spare you from a physical, emotional, or spiritual wound, but an angel of mercy can dress that wound and speed its healing. Angels cannot always help you avoid a path of challenges and obstacles, but angels of mercy can walk beside you and lay rose petals down in front of your next steps.

The angel realm assures me the angels of mercy are an extremely large group of helper angels, large beyond human comprehension, because there is so much suffering in the world. When people think, whisper, or scream prayers of desperation, when humans are crying out or even begging for Spirit's intercession, it is often an angel of mercy who is sent by Spirit to answer these pleas. The angels are showing me pictures of angels of mercy on battlefields, and angels of mercy sitting by hospital beds. Wherever there is poverty, there are angels of mercy. Wherever people are imprisoned, there are angels of mercy. Wherever there are people living in fear or hatred, there are angels of mercy. You may not have money in the bank, but you always have angels of mercy. You may lose your health, but you will never lose the angels of mercy. You may not be able to exercise your freedom, but you can always exercise the mighty influence of the angels of mercy.

The angels have given me an image of a flock of angels of mercy. In this vision they are floating silently but very swiftly to those in need, because the angels of mercy would never make a suffering creature wait a moment for the benefit of their aid and presence. These angels of mercy I see have a very intent, somber look on their faces because they take their jobs so seriously and because often the circumstances of their assignments are so serious. They can feel the intensity of the pain in humans that they are working to alleviate, and angels of mercy take on your problems as if they were their own.

It should be noted that while angels of mercy often intervene in dire, extreme circumstances, you do not have to be at the end of your rope to call upon an angel of mercy. Any time you are facing a challenging situation—from preparing for a difficult talk with a coworker or family member to wanting to make new friends after switching towns or schools—is an ideal occasion to call upon an angel of mercy to bring opportunities, people, and ideas into your life that will make these situations easier and more pleasant. Angels of mercy are "happy," they tell me, to take on any assignment, large or small.

You will feel the presence of these angels and know that they are with you when you experience an undeniable sense of peace despite the circumstances of your crisis, as if the angels of mercy have swooped down, picked you up, and flown you into the calm eye of the storm. Angels of mercy will give you emotional assistance by making you feel at ease, powerful, brave, faithful, sure, worthy, forgiven, or even joyful. Once these angels have wrapped their wings around you, it will feel as if you have been granted sanctuary. They will also give you very practical assistance by sending opportunities, people, and ideas to help you. This might look like suddenly getting a recommendation for the perfect doctor if you are ill, or hearing about the perfect part-time job from a friend if your home is in need of major, expensive repairs. Or the angels might give you ideas about the best way to leave a toxic, abusive relationship, and it is up to you to summon the strength, determination, and faith to act on these nudges from the angels of mercy. If you are having trouble finding this strength, determination, and faith inside yourself, ask the angels of mercy to help you locate or remember it, or ask them if they can lend you some.

Remember that there is nothing that can bar you from the unconditional love and intervention of the angels of mercy. No person or organization or group can stop them from helping you—including yourself. Angels of mercy will assist whether you ask them to or not, whether you believe in them or not. However, the more you call upon them, the more you will be aware of their presence and recognize and therefore be able to act on their guidance. And the more you call upon and acknowledge them, the more you invite the angels of mercy to play a greater role in your life. No matter what you have done or whom you have harmed, the angels of mercy are yours to utilize. You cannot do anything—anything—that will alienate these angels or make them turn their backs—and their wings—on you. The more wretched you feel, and the more cruel your actions, the more they will surround you, trying to convince you of a different way forward and pointing you onto a higher path. Angels of mercy come willingly, eagerly, and equally to all when called. There is no judgment from them regarding you or your situation. Only mercy and—the angels of mercy are asking me to add—forgiveness. The angels of mercy are telling me that they are the angels of second, third, fourth, etc. chances. If you are having trouble forgiving yourself for something, or want help forgiving someone else, ask the angels of mercy to help.

The angels of mercy have a very special request they want me to share with you: More than any other group of helper angels, the angels of mercy need your assistance. Angels often put ideas in our heads and feelings in our hearts about how we can act as human angels. So the next time you get the impulse to make life a little kinder and gentler for someone who is hurting, go ahead and give them a second chance. Help them get back on their feet. Offer them a smile and some encouraging words. Donate to a cause that will benefit them. The angels of mercy will thank you and say a special blessing over your life.

Angel Prayer: Spirit, please remind me that angels of mercy surround me whenever I am scared or in pain, and that I may call on them any time for comfort, grace, healing, and courage.

Angels Are More Like Us than We Think

One of the strongest messages I received from the angel realm while writing this book was also the most surprising: Angels are more like us than we think.

Usually our minds are focused on how *different* angels are. Often angel experts and intuitives talk about how angels are always near, always eager to help. I agree wholeheartedly. One reason angels are able to give so much is because the physical laws that govern heaven are vastly different than the ones that govern earth. The angels are telling me that the easiest way to explain this in terms we can understand is: There are no physical laws in heaven. For example, angels are not run ragged and exhausted by their constant giving and presence in the lives of so many because angels can be everywhere at once.

Anita Moorjani, author of *Dying to Be Me: My Journey from Cancer, to Near Death, to True Healing*, addresses this phenomenon when she talks about her near-death experience. In her lectures, Ms. Moorjani explains how, once she passed over to the other side, she learned that in heaven we are able to be with several loved ones still living at the same time—in other words, watch what they are doing on earth and really be near them, right beside them, as a spiritual presence. One person might be snuggled up in bed fast asleep, while another is busy working at their desk on the other side of the world. Yet once we pass over to heaven we can be with both of these people at the same time. Just like an archangel or ascended master can be with multiple people in different parts of the world at the same time. Ms. Moorjani finds it hard to describe this concept in earthly terms, as it makes no sense here, but according to her it makes perfect sense in heaven and is effortless to execute.

People who've had near-death experiences also relate being whole and healthy in heaven, and seeing relatives who struggled with severe physical limitations on earth in top physical shape and full of energy in heaven. This might be another reason that angels do not get tired or worn out from helping us the same way we might if we attempted to be available to someone twenty-four hours a day. Angels don't have a human body that experiences fatigue and illness. Again, the physical laws that govern earth do not apply in heaven. This is one of the main ways humans and angels differ, and it's a significant difference!

So how are angels like us? I believe angels have hearts and souls just like we do. Although they are not of this earth, and their home is in heaven, a dimension away, the angels are telling me that we should think of them more like the "cousins" of the human race. Shakespeare makes reference to angels shedding tears in *Measure for Measure.* When a character pleads for mercy, she pronounces that man "plays such fantastic tricks before high heaven/ as make the angels weep." And the Bible speaks of angels rejoicing. I too believe that angels are deeply emotional creatures, who experience great joy at our triumphs and great sadness in our despair. A friend asked me if I thought angels felt anger. The angel realm is telling me they feel anger at injustice. The difference is the angels would not take out that anger on the person who perpetrated the injustice, or punish anyone. Would angels try and steer someone toward a more enlightened, loving path? Of course. But an angel's forgiveness is like that of Spirit: immediate, complete, and unconditional. Again, this is another way angels differ from humans. The idea of angels possessing great emotional depth should not come as a shock. Dedicating your existence to helping others certainly requires it. Many angel experts and intuitives say that angels love to hear a thank you for the help they offer. Anyone with a heart would be touched to know that they truly helped someone, and that the person they helped was grateful.

Do angels have distinct, individual personalities? Yes, and identifying your guardian angels' personalities can help you better connect to them. One of my lead guardian angels, Sharon, is very loving and maternal, the ultimate nurturer. I believe

Sharon is the guardian angel I connect with most often because I have abandonment issues from childhood, and Sharon was obviously assigned to me before birth to help me navigate, heal, and address the deep need for love and acceptance that this life has challenged me with. The other guardian angel I connect with often is Samantha, who brings me wisdom and insight from Spirit. Another guardian angel, Windy, is just like her name: a free spirit, and she encourages that part of me that is a free spirit, a wanderer, a loner, an adventurer. Grace is optimistic, holy, and always sees the best in people. And Lucinda is an artistic diva. She cheers on my own artistic endeavors, pushes me to demand the best for myself and of myself, and has a sarcastic sense of humor. You can often get a hint about a guardian angel's personality from their name. My guardian angels are a great team, mainly because each one is unique.

It's easy to think of angels as one-dimensional props that are simply here to grant wishes, send messages to Spirit, or give us love and comfort. Angels *are* all those things. But I believe they are also *far* more dynamic. It's equally easy to focus on the vast differences between humans and angels. But in many key respects we are very similar. That should make you feel more comfortable communicating with angels.

Angel Affirmation: Angels are like humans: endlessly fascinating, deliciously complex, and pure magic.

ANGEL EXERCISE:
ANGEL BLESSING FOR HOMES OR OFFICES

A friend who was going through a rough patch once asked me if I could sense any angels around her. Even before I tried to tune in to my friend and her immediate family members, I was able to assure her that angels were definitely surrounding her, now more than ever in her hour of need.

But since we were sitting on her couch, the two of us alone in her apartment, the soft evening sun setting outside her windows, I decided it was the perfect opportunity to try and ask the angel realm for the names of her guardian angels, as well as the names of the guardian angels of her husband and child. The names of my friend's guardian angels and the guardian angels of her family members came quickly to me. (It's interesting to note that my friend and her husband are of Jewish descent, and the names that came into my mind—both male names—for the guardian angels of her husband and her child are traditional Jewish names.)

Then a voice told me that there was also an angel who was guarding over her house. This communication from the angel realm came as a shock to me, because I hadn't asked for it: I had simply asked for some names of my friends' guardian angels and those of her husband and child. My friend let out a sigh when I told her there was an angel guarding over her house. Somehow this final bit of information from the angel realm made her feel most at ease. She felt she was covered from all angles now!

Since that day on my friend's couch, the angel realm has communicated to me that what I told my friend is not uncommon:

There are angels, probably a sub-group of helper angels, who specialize in protecting and watching over locations such as homes and offices and even woods, lakes, shorelines, oceans, and fields. So it is highly likely that there is an angel who is assigned to guard your home, as well as other guardian angels who are assigned to each member of the family in the home. What do these angels who watch over homes or specific locations do?

The angel realm is telling me that one of the chief tasks of these angels is to keep the energy of the home or space positive and loving—to increase the vibrational energy of the space, bringing it closer to the vibration of Spirit. In a practical sense this could mean family members getting along peacefully or if it is an office space that the work done there is ethical and of exceptional quality (these are outcomes the angels cannot control, only encourage.) The angels have also told me that these helper angels can clean an area. The angels show me an image of angels sweeping out a home with brooms, but what they are sweeping away is not dirt! It is old energy that can accumulate over time: arguments, illnesses, even intense joy and celebration can clutter the energy of a home over time. Your home should feel peaceful, like a safe womb to retreat to. The angels are also telling me that sometimes, probably without the knowledge of the people inhabiting a house, spirits might be hanging out. The angels are showing me an image of a homeless person living on the street in a makeshift cardboard box. That's what these spirits are like—wanderers, sometimes old "ancestors," the angels tell me, of people living in the house. The angels also tell me they may just be spirits who are "lost." Often we will get a sign from a loved one on the other side. These loved ones, as most spirits do, have passed over to heaven and just come to visit us now and again. Popping in to say hi by letting you feel their presence, playing their favorite song on your radio, etc. But these homeless spirits are scared to, or don't know how to, cross over. Usually you never even know these spirits are around, although the angels tell me you might sense that something is "off" about the vibe of the home (this happened to me, and I did, which is rare for me, actually see a ghost in that home later on). But an angel who guards and cleans houses can help these spirits travel to their true home, to heaven.

The following exercise can help maximize or increase the energy of the angel realm in a space you regularly inhabit, as well as clear or reset the general energy of the space. It can be fun to do this exercise if you are moving into a new living space, or if the energy of your office or home feels negative or stagnant. If you perform this angel blessing on an office where there are a lot of other coworkers, it might be best to do it remotely. That way you respect the belief systems of your coworkers (perhaps they are not comfortable with the idea of angels). If you do the exercise remotely, simply picture yourself in the space performing the blessing instead of physically standing in the space as you go about this ritual. I like to perform this ritual with a sage stick. Burning herbs, such as frankincense, in spiritual ceremonies is an ancient practice that has been part of many cultures and spiritual traditions. There is something about smoke, mist, and steam that is mystical and reminds us of Spirit, perhaps because these things appear to magically exist somewhere between the elements of fire, earth, water, and air, just as Spirit seems to be both of this world and not of this world. Sage in particular is known as a purifying agent, used by the ancient Celtic druids and the indigenous people of the Amazon. You can buy sage sticks online or many places where incense is sold. Simply light one and let the smoke fill the space you are purifying. The smell of sage is pungent and distinctive but pleasant (in my opinion). If you can't find a sage stick or don't like the odor of sage, try using any incense stick made of natural herbs—not artificial, chemical perfumes. Using some sort of incense stick adds an element of ancient ritual to this angel blessing, which will increase your ability to be present during the ceremony. Remember, always be mentally alert and responsible when working with anything that must be lit and then put out.

First, make sure you choose a time to do this angel blessing when you will be alone in the space, and there is no danger of interruption for at least half an hour. If you are doing this exercise remotely, simply make sure you can go to a quiet room with a door you can shut as you visualize the space you want to bless. You can either visualize a burning stick of incense or light some incense in the room where you will be doing the visualization.

Go to a corner of the room you want to bless. Wave your sage or incense stick around the area, and as you watch the smoke waft through the air, say, "Divine Spirit, please send an angel to guard over every corner and cranny of this space, and keep the energy of this space supportive, inspiring, and loving. Let this angel keep the people who live in, work in, or simply visit this space, safe and healthy. Let this angel help purify their hearts and minds, and finally let this angel bring them closer to you."

Feel free to add your own message as well. You can personalize this angel blessing by listing the names of the people who inhabit this space, or you can list some of your specific concerns (maybe someone in the space is ill and needs extra support, healing, and positive energy, or perhaps two people in the space have been at odds recently and you hope an angel can help them work out their differences or clear some of the negative energy this bickering has left behind).

Repeat this angel blessing in each corner of the room you want to bless, or if you are blessing a large space with many rooms, you can simply stand in the middle of each room and perform the blessing. At times you may sense that an area of a room, or a whole room, has a thick energy that needs extra clearing. If so, simply stay in that room, waving your incense stick carefully and safely, a bit longer before moving on.

When you have blessed each corner or room of this space, you can carefully put out your sage or incense stick. Sit cross-legged or in a comfortable position in the center of the space or in the center of the main room of the space.

Close your eyes. Visualize an angel flying down from heaven, through the stars and the clouds and finally landing softly on the roof of this space. This angel has enormous wings, wings that are as big as the space itself. The angel wraps both of these wings around the space and settles in on the roof, like a momma bird settles into its nest. This angel is here to stay, here to support and protect this space and everyone in it.

Close the blessing by thanking the angel realm for clearing the energy of your space, and thank the angel who is now watching over the space.

2

What Can Angels Do for Us, and What Are Their Limitations?

Often there is confusion about the role of the angel realm in our earthly life. Sometimes this confusion can even lead humans to feel abandoned or forgotten by the angels, which I assure you is *never* the case.

Why are some prayers seemingly not answered? Why do angels appear to intervene in some situations and not others? Why don't angels spare us from every tragedy? Do angels help humans even when we don't ask for help? What is the nature of our relationship to angels on a spiritual level? How do the angels relate to each other? Does Spirit have a set plan for our life? Are there aspects of our life path that we can negotiate with

Spirit and the help of the angel realm? Does our highest good, which the angels always lead us toward, always *feel* good? Are there ways that humans can invite the angels to play a larger role in our lives?

We'll discuss all these exciting questions and more in this chapter. At the end of it I hope you feel inspired, comforted, and curious. Most of all, I hope you will have a clearer understanding of how to best utilize all the resources the angel realm has to offer.

Fate, Free Will, and the Angel Realm

Your guardian angels want you to understand one of the most powerful dichotomies of earthly existence: fate and free will. There are certain aspects of your life that were fated, or planned out, before you were even born. Some of these are obvious: What family you were born into. Your cultural and racial heritage. The color of your eyes and hair. But did you know that much more than that was mapped out for you before you were born? Jobs you will hold, and certainly your callings. Archetypes inside you—like student, healer, mother, performer—that will be activated at specific times and via specific events? Challenges you will face, important relationships you will have—many of these unique aspects of your life were set in motion when you were still residing with the angels in the world of Spirit.

The knowledge that much of life is preordained can feel comforting. It's not all chaos! There's a path, lessons to be learned, rhyme and reason, a grand design or purpose to it all. And other times this notion of fate can feel stifling, suffocating. That's when it's time to contemplate, and exercise, your free will.

Like a big vacation, much of your human journey has been carefully researched and planned ahead of time by your soul, your soul family, your spirit guides, your guardian angels, and Spirit itself. Yet how you experience that journey, and the details of the journey, are up to you. What will you make of these relationships you'll experience? How much will you work on self-improvement? How much love will you give away? How gentle and kind will you be toward yourself? How far will you take your potential as an artist or teacher? How will you mentor the children in your life? What career choices will you make? How will you heal from an illness, and how long will it take? Will you accept the help that Spirit sends? Will you rush through life or savor it? Will you stop to reflect and learn lessons or will you repeat the same mistakes over and over? Will you make the journey as difficult and unforgiving as possible, or will you make the journey as comfortable and joyous as possible? Where will you take risks and when will you play it safe?

Your guardian angels want you to know that so much of how you experience and interpret this journey is up to you, via the choices you make with your free will. That can feel liberating, but it can also feel intimidating. Relax—you're not alone. Your guardian angels will be right there every step of the way, encouraging you through the signs and people they send, and through your own intuition, to help you make the best choices.

Your angels want you to have the most rewarding life possible. Your angels want you to make gutsy decisions that allow you to live up to your full potential. Your angels want you to protect yourself and create stability so you have a safe foundation from which to take off and soar. Your angels want you to recognize and accept the grace and aid Spirit offers during times of crisis and transition. Your angels want you to celebrate and experience all the joy and wonder life has to offer.

Your guardian angels want you to know that others, naturally, have free will as well. You might cry out to Spirit, "Please, don't take my husband from me!" But if your husband wants a divorce, wants to leave you, that decision is, "largely," the angels tell me, up to him. Angels cannot interfere with another person's free will, even, the angels inform me, if they desperately want to. If they feel someone is about to take an action against their best interests—say, if your husband is acting rashly—angels can try and dissuade the person from taking action. But ultimately we all have free will, and it's a mighty powerful force. The angels are reminding me that humans are powerful spiritual beings and free will is one of the main ways we exercise that power. It is a gift from Spirit, meant to be used, not usurped. The exception to this is if you are going to do something with your free will that goes expressly against your life path, the life path of another, or the will of Spirit. Then, in some cases, the angels can intervene in dramatic ways. More likely they will put up roadblocks to try and stop you from taking the path you're currently headed down. If something doesn't work out over and over, it might simply be that this aspect of your journey is meant to be challenging. Not all things are intended to be easy! But it might indicate that angels and Spirit are putting up roadblocks to get you to abandon this path and consider another. If you get quiet and ask the angels, you should be able to tell the difference.

Your guardian angels are here to drop breadcrumbs along the path, leading you through this earthly trip via the most advantageous route. A route of self-love, self-expression, service, wisdom, joy, and gratitude. The angels want you to watch for signposts from them along the journey. They lead you to advantageous choices and opportunities that facilitate the most dynamic version of the life you signed up for in heaven.

You could also think of your earthly existence as a dinner invitation your soul accepted. The restaurant is set. Your dinner companions are assigned. The time of your reservation is already on the books. That is all fated. But what will you wear? What will you order when the waiter hands you the menu? What will you discuss over the main course? Will you have coffee afterward and linger? Will you have dessert? Will you tip well? These are all matters of free will.

Free will and fate are like peanut butter and chocolate. Strawberries and cream. A burger and fries. Each element is good on its own, but they are so much better when paired. Together fate and free will balance each other out. Together fate and free will transcend to become something special, extraordinary.

How does your free will influence your relationship with the angel realm? The angel realm will support and guide you whether you acknowledge angels or not. Take your guardian angels, for example. It is their fate to help you. They will always be offering you love and comfort and guidance. However, the more you ask for their help, the more active a role they will play in your life—the more guidance they will offer, the more you will feel their presence. That's because you are saying to the angels, "Hey, guys, I want more of you in my life!" This is your free will being exercised. When I asked the angel realm to show me a way to express how human free will works with the angel realm, they sent me an image of a flower being watered. Simply put, the more you communicate with the angel realm and acknowledge the presence of angels, the more your relationship with the angel realm will grow, just like a plant that is watered and well cared for will grow and flourish.

Your angels want you to understand fate and exercise free will to help you make the most of this soul assignment called earthly life. When both fate and free will are working harmoniously, it's a recipe for alchemy. It's how humans turn an ordinary existence into spiritual gold.

Angel Prayer: Guardian angels, grant me the serenity to accept the things I cannot change, the courage to change the things I can, and the wisdom to know the difference.

You Have Soul Contracts with Your Guardian Angels

A book about angels is an appropriate place to discuss soul contracts, since you have important soul contracts with each of your guardian angels. I was introduced to the concept of soul contracts by soul contract astrologer and intuitive life strategist Robert

Ohotto. Robert is a progressive author, radio show host, and professional intuitive with a fun bedside manner.

I believe that soul contracts are agreements you made with angels, spirit guides, relatives, coworkers, friends, institutions, places, and even Spirit itself before you were born. Your guardian angels have soul contracts with you wherein they agreed to guide and protect you throughout this lifetime, and possibly other lifetimes as well. Some soul contracts are what would be considered minor, and/or may only span a short period of time. Others, like the ones with your guardian angels, are significant in content and length.

Do you have a very close friend whom you've known since you were a child, or one you have stayed close with throughout your adult life? Even though you aren't family, you might think of each other more like siblings than friends. That's because you are soul siblings. No doubt you both entered into a soul contract with each other before you were born. Soul contracts are often made with people in our soul family, souls we were close with on the other side and have perhaps shared past lives with. What did you and your good friend agree to help each other with in this life? You can get clues to the details of your soul contract by examining things like: when you met, important lessons you have taught each other over the years, challenges you have helped each other overcome. You've probably learned much from this person and been greatly nourished by the relationship. It's hard to look back on your life and imagine it without these soul siblings. I have a friend like this named Cathryn who has been a key part of my life for over two decades. Just hearing her voice on the telephone makes me feel so grounded, so *myself*. I'm sure we planned several details of our relationship (where and when we would meet, ways we would challenge and support and inspire each other) before we were even born. With people like this there is often a strong connection right away. You can talk to them about anything, you get along remarkably well, you may be struck by them the first time you see them—before you even get a chance to speak. Or you might have a strong negative reaction to them: find them incredibly rude or boring. Many times this negative initial impression changes to a positive one as you get to know the person. Or perhaps this negative initial impression later proves to have been a warning that this person is someone you should steer clear of in this life. I think a strong initial reaction, one way or another, is always worth examining for a possible soul connection.

Other soul contracts are only meant to handle a specific event or issue and are short in duration. Do you have a friendship or work relationship where you learned something significant from someone, but then the relationship naturally ended, or you felt it was time to move on? This was probably still a soul contract, made before you were born, but you weren't meant to be a major player in the life of this particular soul. Perhaps you've had past lives together but always chose to be supporting as opposed to starring roles in each other's lives. Or maybe you had a heavy and lengthy soul contract with this person in a past life and now you are sitting out the drama for a second!

(A quick note on past lives: Having past lives is something that resonates strongly with me personally. I know past lives may not resonate with all people who believe in angels, yet I think past lives are worth discussing briefly in this section. If you'd like to know more about past-life theories, there are tons of books out there that can discuss the concept in greater depth.)

I believe you can also have soul contracts with souls you only know casually on the other side, souls who are not part of your soul family, and souls whom you have never met in a past life. Say for instance that you agree with Spirit to go through a certain challenge while you are on earth. Perhaps you agree to have a certain disease so you can help others heal, learn something on a soul level during your own healing, or teach others what you learn during your journey managing this condition. Another soul in heaven might say something like, "Hi! Spirit let me know what you are planning. I'm going to be down on earth when you're there, helping people with that same disease. I really dig the way you will learn and grow and help others via this experience. I want to draft a soul contract to be your doctor."

I don't personally believe we always have soul contracts with people who help us. I think sometimes a problem or need arises in our lives and our guardian angels look around, see who is available and appropriate and send that person to us for the mutual benefit of both people.

Other soul contracts you might have are with some of your helper angels, who agree to step in at certain predetermined points in your life when you have a need for their particular area of discipline. You may have a soul contract with an archangel if your soul purpose has a particular need for that archangel's specialty. Likewise I think you can have soul contracts with some of your spirit guides and ascended masters.

You also have an elaborate soul contract with Spirit itself. This details things you agreed to experience, teach, and learn here on earth during your lifetime. Are these contracts negotiable? I believe so, to a degree. It's hard to negotiate things you aren't aware of, and I feel that many items in these contracts are not known to our conscious minds. But I do believe some things can be negotiated, and that's a great time to get your guardian angels involved. You can tell them: "Hey, I don't know if I signed up for what I'm experiencing right now, but I really want to see if there is a way to change or modify our agreement on this one." Maybe you have one child, but later in life decide you'd like a second. You try to conceive but can't. You look into adoption but it's more than you can afford. Ask your angels to help. You can write a journal entry to your angels, asking them to explain to everyone in heaven that you really feel a second child is right for your family, and you want some guidance and help to achieve this. Then watch for messages from your angels in the form of thoughts and feelings and even people and opportunities regarding this issue of a second child. There is an interesting movie that deals with this exact question of whether we can negotiate aspects of our fate with Spirit called *The Adjustment Bureau.* I was fascinated when I saw the film, and then later I heard Robert Ohotto mention the movie on his radio show and I knew I was on to something!

Certain aspects of our existence are obviously nonnegotiable: your natural eye color, the family you were born into. And while I believe other aspects are negotiable, I think some that could possibly be negotiable are often not (like wanting someone to be your life partner yet having the relationship never work out or the other person feel differently). But as you know, it never hurts to ask your angels to get involved. Even if something cannot be shifted, your angels are excellent at giving you intuitive wisdom about why some things are best left as they are.

What happens when a soul contract is up? Sometimes relationships we're in and roles we play will leave our lives peacefully and easily. Other times there's a big blowup and lots of drama. Both types of endings may signal the completion of a soul contract. Some soul contracts might be very important to your journey, but be relatively brief. An example is when two people get married and immediately have a child, but then quickly get divorced. Often the couple never completely regrets getting together because they created such a wonderful little person. They see there was a purpose to their union, but they also realize that they were not meant to be life partners. The soul contract was to have a child together and be co-parents, but that's it.

Sometimes life will create little dramas to help you leave a situation or relationship if your soul contract is up but you are having trouble walking away on your own. An example of this might be getting fired or laid off from your job. We can have soul contracts with organizations, and you might have had one with a company you worked for. Say you worked there for many years and were a faithful employee. You gained much from the experience. Maybe you've thought about leaving, and daydreamed about a different career, but were too scared to walk away. The job might end simply because your soul contract there is up, and it's time for you to start a new career.

This is a good time to note that you should never be afraid to walk away from an abusive or toxic situation or relationship because you feel you will be betraying a soul contract. Taking good care of yourself and setting healthy boundaries trumps all, and your angels always want you to be safe.

If you feel you have an important soul contract regarding a relationship or situation in your life, it can be fun and insightful to ask your guardian angels to give you intuitive hints about the nature and length of this particular contract. I'm also being guided to tell you that another option is employing a helper angel who specializes in soul contract "law." These particular helper angels are very astute and organized and are expert researchers. I'm seeing an image of one in a library wearing glasses, and this angel is surrounded by books and papers that no doubt contain your soul contracts and those of everyone and everything you are linked with. These soul contract helper angels are detail-oriented, and very eager to share their expertise with us!

Angel Prayer: Angels, please help me see all the roles I play and relationships I'm in from a spiritual perspective, and help me remember that many of them were planned out before I was born.

Angels Are Action Heroes

We've all heard stories about angels swooping in and saving the day in dramatic ways. People have reported angels healing them, angels saving them from drowning, angels scaring away attackers and thieves. It's fun to think of angels as action heroes. But more than wanting you to think of angels as action heroes, angels want you to see yourself as an action hero. While it's true that angels may intervene and pull our chestnuts out of the fire when a situation is dire, more often angels give us guidance about action steps that we can take to save ourselves.

When you pray to an angel for help or guidance, don't assume that means an angel is going to come in and fix everything for you. In fact, that is very rarely the case. Usually an angel's help will arrive in the form of thoughts or feelings about action steps you can take to improve the situation yourself. Another way an angel will help is to send opportunities or people into your life. Again, it is up to you to utilize these opportunities and engage these people.

If angels are so loving and so powerful, why don't angels just fold us up in their wings and take care of everything for us? Because we came to earth from the world of Spirit so that we could do big things here. You are a spirit starring in this human drama, and your role is to grow as a soul and help heal the planet and its inhabitants. That's gonna mean some intense scenes! Cue the action montage! This is not a passive part you signed on for—you're not an extra milling about in the background waiting for the catering truck to arrive. And it's too late to call your agent and back out. You're here, the curtain has gone up, and the rest of us need you to take your place center stage.

An angel rescuing you every time you need help would rob you of learning many of the lessons your soul agreed to experience here. And robbing you of those lessons further robs others of what you would have been able to teach. An angel doesn't come in and save you for the same reason a mother doesn't always jump in and save her child. She wants the child to learn to do for themselves. Spirit and the angels also want you to learn to do for yourself.

The angels have guided me to share a dramatic example of this from the book *Unbroken: A World War II Story of Survival, Resilience and Redemption* by the talented storyteller Laura Hillenbrand. This bestseller is the true account of Louie Zamperini, an Army Air Corpsman whose B-24 was shot down by the Japanese. Louie spent forty-seven days on a life raft in shark-infested waters. At some point during that terrible voyage on the raft, Louie's exhausted, sunburnt, gaunt face looked up to the sky and witnessed a miracle: A group of human figures floated high above his raft. (The angels are asking me to tell you that some of the most profound miracles you will witness will come during your darkest hours.) Louie counted twenty-one of these divine angels hovering above him, and "they were singing the sweetest song he had ever heard." I believe with all my heart, as does Louie, that what he saw and heard was not a hallucination. I believe it was an actual group of angels—no doubt Louie's guardian angels among them. These angels let Louie know, by allowing Louie to see and hear them, that he had not been abandoned. No doubt angels also gave Louie some of the ideas he had that kept himself and his fellow soldier on the raft alive: the rationing of food, how to filter seawater for drinking, how to evade the sharks, catching and eating birds, etc. However it was up to Louie and his friend to execute these ideas and make it through this ordeal. Why didn't the angels save them and spare them this nightmare? The answer is complex, involving the free will of the people engaged in this war, the soul contracts of those people, and the "dark forces" (this is the description the angels asked me to use) at work in the world that brought this war about, but a big piece of the puzzle is that Louie would use surviving this experience to inspire millions of people—including me. People all over the world battling illnesses, despair, injustice—they have been inspired by Louie and his story to keep going. They have also been inspired to be kinder to others and to forgive people who hurt them because of Louie's tale. To accomplish all that, Louie had to first *have* this experience.

Thankfully Louie's experience is not an everyday one for most people. But it does illustrate that the angels want you to take more action on your own behalf, whether the circumstances you're in are everyday or crisis level or even catastrophic. When you do take action, you often realize you didn't need someone else, like an angel, to swoop in and save you. You are a dynamic spiritual being and capable of far more than you realize. You are stronger and wiser than you imagine. And remember, your angels will be with you every step of the way as you take action, sending you guidance and courage and cheering you on. Say yes to more opportunities. Get more involved in your relationships. If there's something you're unhappy with in your life, ask your angels for guidance, listen to your gut about action steps, and then take action. If there's something you want to change about the world, figure out what action steps you as an individual can take to make a difference.

Angels are superheroes—and you're a superhero too.

Angel Prayer: Angels, show me which action steps are most appropriate for me to take in my life right now.

When Angels Warn You

Angels can't always warn you when something bad is about to happen. Some pain in life cannot be avoided, and it is part of the journey you signed up for before you came here, part of the growing and learning and healing your soul will go through during its time on this planet. For everything else—all those fender benders and tears and frustrations that don't have to happen—your angels will often try to warn you ahead of time to save you headache and heartbreak.

Your angels can warn you through any of the normal methods they use to contact you (see chapter three). The most common way angels warn us is through our gut instinct. You might meet a potential business partner for the first time and get an uneasy feeling about this person (you don't go through with the deal, and later hear from a friend that this potential partner's business went under or that they acted unethically). Or you might be saying good-bye to your spouse as they leave for work in the morning and get the feeling you should make sure they aren't forgetting their phone (your partner tells you it was a good thing you reminded them to take it, because they had to make an important call on their train ride to work). You might be fighting with a loved one, and just before you are about to speak you get the strong sense that you should shut your mouth (you ignore the feeling, and end up saying something you regret that hurts your loved one deeply).

Another common way you might get a warning from an angel is by hearing an angel's voice: "Don't go in there!" or "Wait for the next train" or "Show up early for that appointment" or "Smile at him." Dreams are also a place where angels can issue warnings. You might dream that if you handle a situation the way you are planning to, it will go badly (better come up with plan number two). Or you might have a dream where a friend confesses they are in love with you (if you don't return these feelings, it could be a warning to be careful with your friend's heart, or that you need to address the situation).

Your guardian angels' job is to make sure you have the best version of the life you signed up for. One way they do this is to warn you when you are about to make a decision or take an action that will cause you or someone else needless pain. Think of your life as an old-fashioned train trip. Back when trains were the major mode of long-distance transportation, there were different places to sit on the train based on how expensive a ticket you could afford (this is still true, but long ago the differences between sections were more pronounced). You might sit in first class, coach, or freight (this is when you hop on for free and ride the rails—gets the job done, but it ain't comfortable).

The good news is that you are always entitled to a seat in the first-class version of your life. The first-class version of your life is where you will live your highest potential and experience the most growth, excitement, and pleasure. Whether your journey is first class or not depends largely on the choices you make, and one of those choices is whether or not you will heed your angels' warnings. Your angels are divine conductors always leading you to a seat in first class, but you may choose not to follow.

So what happens when you don't listen to your angels' warnings? Try not to beat yourself up for ignoring a warning. We all sometimes ignore that gut feeling, and then look back later and wish we would have paid attention to it. The important thing is to do a better job of heeding a warning the next time, because the more you pay attention to angelic guidance and your own intuition, the stronger both will become. Recently I had an angel warn me continually about something, and I ignored each and every warning! I was looking for something to increase my chances of conception, and thought I'd found a product that would do the trick. I read reviews online from other customers who used the product with quick, dramatic results. "You don't need it," a voice in my head said. I knew this was one of my guardian angels. But I was so excited about the positive reviews, and so desperate to get pregnant, I bought the product anyway. As I was purchasing the product online, one of my angels repeated, "You don't need it." Of course I bought it anyway. When the product came in the mail, I opened it and heard: "You don't need it." You guessed it—I tried it anyway. My angels were right—while this product had worked for other people, it did nothing for me. I had ignored my angel's repeated warnings because I was so obsessed with accomplishing this goal, and so frustrated that it wasn't happening. After I realized I'd wasted time and money on this product, I felt more frustrated than ever, more desperate than ever (my angels wanted to spare me this). I was definitely experiencing the freight-car version of my life! I got quiet and asked why I was having trouble getting pregnant. "Timing," an angelic voice in my head said. This is what I had suspected, and one of my guardian angels had just confirmed it: The timing wasn't right at this moment for what I was trying to bring into my life. I'd have to wait it out until the stars aligned.

Angel Affirmation: I am open to warnings from my angels and try to heed them. But when I don't, there is no need to punish myself. I can simply ask my angels for more guidance about the next right step.

Asking Your Guardian Angels to Communicate with Other Guardian Angels

Do guardian angels hang out with other guardian angels? I picture a celestial cafe where guardian angels can sit and rest their wings, unwind after a hard day, trade stories, and relax. Angels can most certainly communicate with each other, and one request you can make of your guardian angels is that they communicate with the guardian angels of someone you know on your behalf.

If you are going to a job interview, you might ask your guardian angels to speak to the guardian angels of the person conducting the interview. Your request could sound something like, "Dear guardian angels, please ask the guardian angels of the person conducting my interview tomorrow to make sure this interviewer is open to me as a candidate. Please ask the interviewer's guardian angels to help the interviewer see all my strengths, my enthusiasm, and my willingness to work hard." Your request should *not* sound like this: "Dear guardian angels, please ask the interviewer's guardian angels to convince the interviewer that I'm the best candidate they have ever encountered. Please ask the interviewer's guardian angels to convince the interviewer not to consider anyone else for the job, and to hire me on the spot." Do you see the difference between these two requests? One asks only that the interviewer see the candidate for who the candidate really is, and that the interviewer be open to that candidate as a real possibility. The other request tries to control and manipulate the situation in a way that may not work out for the highest good of the interviewer, the candidate making the prayer request, or anyone else applying for the job.

Guardian angels cannot control the free will of another person for your benefit. Nor should they. Our free will is a divine gift we are all blessed with. Also, your guardian angels are always working for your highest good, and getting this job simply may not be for your highest good. Yet asking that the interviewer sees your strengths and seriously considers you can't hurt anything, and is something your guardian angels can influence by speaking to the interviewer's guardian angels. Other appropriate requests might be, "Please let the interviewer be in a good mood tomorrow" or "Please let the interviewer get a good night's sleep."

Occasionally I will ask my guardian angels to speak to my husband's guardian angels if we've had a fight or can't get on the same page about an important issue. A request of this nature might go something like: "Dear guardian angels, please speak to my husband's guardian angels. Please ask my husband's guardian angels to help my husband listen to me and see things from my point of view. Ask that his guardian angels help my husband have an open mind and not make any quick judgments. Ask his guardian angels to help my husband be open to a compromise so we can both be happy and feel like our needs are being met." The following request is something I would never ask—no matter how badly I sometimes want to! "Dear guardian angels, please speak to my husband's guardian angels and get them to convince my husband that I am right. Ask that his guardian angels make my husband feel eager to please me and follow my lead." I'm sure you're getting the idea!

You can ask your guardian angels to speak to the guardian angels of anyone in your life: a coworker, a family member, a friend, an authority figure. One popular way to use this technique is for finding a romantic partner. The fantastic angel author Doreen Virtue often encourages her single fans to write a letter to their soul mate's guardian angels. It doesn't matter that you probably have not met this future romantic partner yet. Many of the major loves of your life are already written in the stars, so your guardian angels will know where to look to find the guardian angels of your next romantic partner. Your letter to your guardian angels might explain why you want a romantic partner, some of the traits that are important to you in a romantic partner, and how much you want to have a relationship. This is a powerful activation of your free will, basically deputizing your angels to bring love into your life. Besides possibly speeding up the meeting of two people who are fated to be lovers, I believe this can enable guardian angels to canvas other guardian angels to see if there is someone suited to you who is also ready to be in a relationship and fits your current life journey. I don't believe that all relationships are written in the stars—there is always room for improvisation in our lives. (Keep in mind that meeting a soul mate can be largely about divine timing. You might also ask the angels if there is anything you need to work on first that would help you prepare for and attract a healthy relationship into your life.)

Angels are always happy to collaborate on your behalf, and asking your guardian angels to speak to the guardian angels of someone else gives the angels an opportunity to do even more teamwork.

Angel Affirmation: I can always ask my guardian angels to contact another person's guardian angels on my behalf. When guardian angels work in teams, miracles happen.

Place a Dessert Order
with Your Guardian Angels

Now that you're learning more about your angels, who they are and all that they can do for you, it might be an appropriate moment to ground yourself in an essential fact: Angels are not genies in a bottle. They cannot grant every wish. They cannot spare you every pain.

Your guardian angels want you to have the best life possible. That's why they are always listening for your prayers and sending you guidance. It's why they are constantly working behind the scenes up in heaven as negotiators and diplomats on your behalf, trying to broker the best deal they can for you in this life between what Spirit wants for you, what your soul family wants for you, what your own soul wants for you, and even what that cute, determined little ego of yours wants for you too.

Angels are like spiritual waiters. You see something you like on the menu of life and give an angel your order. Next the angel goes about offering you guidance on action steps you should take regarding this wish. Maybe one of your guardian angels talks to the angels of some people who could help you, and then sends those people into your life. One of your angels might scan the opportunities available to you and send what will be, from their angel's eye view, the best-possible opportunity in the long run. And remember, your guardian angels are doing all this while integrating your current desire into your broader life purpose and destiny, as well as considering the free will and destinies of others—all that heavy stuff. The upshot is: Angels can't make something happen simply because you ask them for it.

Nothing is ever given to you, or denied you, by Spirit as a punishment. Your guardian angels want you to know that just because they can't always give you what you desire, that doesn't mean that your angels love you any less. When a prayer isn't answered the way you want, it does not mean your angels have forgotten or abandoned you.

You can't always get what you want. But to help the medicine of life go down, your guardian angels want you to know that there is one thing you can always order and receive: dessert.

Dessert defines all those little treats in life that are available to everyone at anytime. You may be denied things, but you will never be denied dessert—aka life's little mercies. You will know something is "dessert" because it will have a sweetness to it. Your guardian angel may not be able to secure that big grant you applied for to fund your work project, but your guardian angel can send you a phone call from your best friend out of the blue right after you receive the bad news, a phone call that makes you feel inspired and comforted. A phone call you treasure. A phone call that suddenly makes you feel glad to be alive. That's dessert, and your life always has room for it.

It pains your guardian angels to see you confused or hurt or discouraged when a prayer is not answered as hoped, and when you feel this way your guardian angels want it to become an automatic trigger for you to treat yourself to something special, to nurture yourself in a deliberate way. Think "dessert" with these treats: rich, decadent, spoiling. It doesn't have to be expensive, but it has to be an indulgence. Something that makes you want to clap or squeal or do a little dance just at the thought of it. Something that gives you a break from big goals, and brings back that pure joy of living in the moment. That is dessert. Dessert might be sent your way by a guardian angel—like getting a coupon in the mail for a free massage after you've come home from a crummy day at the office. Or your angels might nudge you to treat yourself, giving you the idea to call in for a "staying at home well" day. Other fun ways you can treat yourself: A long walk through your favorite spot in nature. A picnic with a friend. A last-minute romantic dinner out with your partner. A splurge at your favorite store. Asking or hiring someone to do the spring cleaning for you. Taking yourself and a girlfriend to lunch or to get a facial. Blowing off chores or leaving work early to spend the afternoon playing basketball with a friend or your kids. A walk with your loved one along the beach or boardwalk at night. Star gazing on a park bench. Putting off homework or a freelance assignment to binge read a great book or binge watch a great show. Buying yourself flowers.

Next time you feel disappointed because you asked for your angels' help with something, went out and tried your best, and things didn't work out the way you hoped or expected, ask your guardian angels for dessert. You might say a prayer like: "Dear guardian angels, I've had the wind taken out of my sails. This situation didn't shape up like I prayed. I tried my best, and I know you did the best you could for me, but it just wasn't meant to be. I can't help but feel disappointed. Can you send me something special for dessert?" Then be on the lookout for people or invitations or gifts that might have been sent as treats from your angels. Angels love dessert, and they're good at baking it and serving it too. When you get your sweet treat from the angels, or they send you inspiration via a thought or a feeling about a way you can go out and treat yourself, it will remind you that your angels do care, and that they are always listening. Just because everything you ask isn't given, doesn't mean angels aren't right there taking the orders.

Your angels hate to see you crushed and discouraged. They would shield you from all pain if they could, but they can't. That's simply not what this life is about. Letting your angels serve you a squeal-worthy dessert is like letting a mother bandage a child's knee after a scrape. You'll feel better when you order dessert, and so will your angels.

Angel Affirmation: Just because I didn't get what I asked for does not mean I am being punished or abandoned by my angels. I can always ask them to treat me to a special dessert just to feel their presence and remind me that I am loved.

Where Are Angels When Tragedy Strikes?

When our world falls apart because a loved one is taken from us, or we're left quaking in the aftermath of an act of extreme violence, we might find ourselves asking, "Where were the angels?" As I discuss throughout this book, there are many spiritual factors in play during a tragedy: the fate of the people involved, their free will and the free will of others, the intention each of these souls had when they came to earth regarding what they wanted to experience and accomplish here. Another very important piece of the puzzle is how the tragedy will affect, both negatively and positively, every individual, institution, and culture that the event touches. That said, we might never fully understand why a tragedy was allowed to happen, and even having faith in a spiritual "bigger picture" in the wake of a tragedy does not lessen our grief or outrage, or even our anger at Spirit.

We know that angels can intervene in our lives in dramatic ways: appearing as a stranger who shuts down a piece of heavy machinery just before it injures us, whispering in our ear to take a different train or driving route so we avoid a fatal collision, pulling us from a burning building just before the roof collapses. But what the angel realm desperately wants us to understand is that there are times when angels are not allowed to intervene. Again, this is due to a complex set of circumstances that we will examine many times in this book. So, if angels are not allowed to intervene in the tragic death of an individual, the question remains: "Where were the angels when all this tragedy was unfolding?"

As I finished the final edits of this book, a horrific act of violence was committed in Charleston, South Carolina, that took many innocent lives. The day after nine parishioners at Emanuel African Methodist Episcopal Church, a historic house of worship and political activism for the African American community in Charleston, were shot and killed, I asked myself this very question: "Where were the angels?" While I and the entire country experienced rage, sorrow, confusion, and indignation,

I assumed that this must have been a situation where the angels' wings were tied, for reasons we can guess at but may never fully comprehend or even be able to accept. Surely, if the angels could have intervened to save those nine precious lives, they would have. I believe strongly that the angels were giving the shooter messages that what he was planning was terribly wrong. Angels can try to convince someone that the path they are on is dangerous, and in their own way angels will try to talk someone around, tirelessly, by sending signs, gut feelings, and thoughts. Sadly, as in this case, people do not always listen to angelic guidance. And if the angels weren't allowed to intervene in a more dramatic way in this situation, what exactly were they up to at the hour this dark event was taking place? We know what they did leading up to it: tried to convince the shooter not to do this, and surely even tried to give friends and family members clues that the shooter was planning something awful. But what did the angels do next?

After working with angels for so many years, I should have known the answer to that question, because I know that there is one thing you can always count on with angels: They will never abandon you. It doesn't matter where you are, or what you've done, angels are always at your side, especially during the most trying moments of your life. But I think my mind was so blown by the enormity of this cruel, sinister mass murder that I needed the angels to walk me through it from their perspective.

The angels immediately sent me answers, through images, feelings, and intuitive knowing. First, the angels want you to comprehend that when something like this happens they are feeling the exact same emotions as the people who are suffering. The angels shared with me their emotional experience when they saw the shooter walk into that church. With video surveillance cameras, the police had a clear image of the shooter as he entered the church. Because this image was circulated to the public in order to identify and capture the shooter, it was this moment that came to mind when I queried the angels.

The angels felt pure terror, dread, and extreme anxiety when the shooter entered the building. They tell me they were hoping "right up until the end" that this wouldn't happen. I am told by the angel realm that not only were there "thousands" (this is the number the angels gave me when I asked how many angels were present) of angels at the church directly before, during, and after the shooting, but the guardian angels of every parishioner inside were surrounding their charges. These guardian angels stayed by the sides of the people they love and are sworn to protect. I got an image of an angel with his hands on the shoulders of one of the people who was killed in the church. Not only were these guardian angels with their charges at the time of the attack, but they were literally holding on to them.

And the shooter? The angel realm informed me that when someone who has committed actions like this dies and reaches the other side, they will be made to feel all the pain and fear that each of their victims and those connected to them felt because of their actions. This will be done not so much as a punishment, but as a lesson for the soul. It will in effect be a terrible, harrowing experience. The angels are telling me that this is what hell is. Hell is not a place, but an "experience," the angels say. A temporary experience on the other side, in heaven, where each of us feels the emotional cost of all our actions here on earth. I have also received information from the angel realm that while offenders like the Charleston shooter are in the midst of experiencing the nightmarish consequences of their actions in heaven, there will be angels and an ascended master by their side, and that ascended master will be Jesus. What do the angels want us to gain from this knowledge I am sharing? That there is "no end to the mercy and unconditional love," the angels tell me, on the other side of this life. It is true for absolutely everyone. That includes you, as well as the most deranged and dangerously mentally ill among us.

The angels showed me through images that they too weep during these kinds of events. Even when angels are not able to intervene in a dramatic way, they desperately want to. They feel your pain as their own. When angels cannot prevent a tragedy, they stand with us, often holding on to us tight, waiting at the ready until the moment they take us back home to heaven.

As we already touched on, one way that angels will participate in a tragedy when they are not allowed to simply prevent it is to encourage humans to act angelically. Angels will convince someone, by putting thoughts in their mind and feelings in their heart, to act on the angel realm's behalf. And sometimes people actually listen! The angels have told me that this was the case with Willem Arondeus, a resistance fighter in the Netherlands during World War II.

[1]Willem was not Jewish, but he was sympathetic to the unthinkable suffering the Jewish people were enduring during this time. Living openly as a homosexual in a period in history when being honest about such things was taboo at best and life-threatening at worst, Willem knew what it was like to be unfairly persecuted for simply being yourself. And as a homosexual he knew what it was like to be one of the people the Nazis were committed to exterminating.

But saving himself was not Willem's main motivation when he joined a unit of the Resistance that falsified papers for Dutch Jews to hide their Jewish ancestry from the Nazis. In 1943, Willem led his unit in an attack on an Amsterdam registry office, setting it on fire to destroy records against which false identity papers he had created for Dutch Jews could be checked. Thousands of files were destroyed, and many Jewish lives saved. Days later Willem and his unit were betrayed, arrested, and executed. The angels are telling me that this outcome "was a risk Willem was willing to take." The angels say Willem had that "fighter" or "warrior" spirit. Like Martin Luther King Jr., Willem was willing to risk his life fighting for what he knew was right. The Vikings believed that those who died in combat were received in Valhalla, and I believe there is a special section in heaven for those who die fighting for what is right.

Willem saw something very wrong happening in the world, found a way to do something about it, and was willing to risk his

---

1   United States Holocaust Memorial Museum (ushmm.org)

life for another group of people. The angel realm is informing me that Willem was very "bighearted"—that's the exact word the angels gave me. An incredibly ethical person who was very concerned with standing up for what is right. This was the perfect person for the angels to encourage to act in a heroic, compassionate, protective way on their behalf. Is it any wonder that his last name, Arondeus, contains the word *deus*, the Latin word for God?

When angels are not allowed to intervene in tragedies directly, they often look to bighearted people and inspire them to get in touch with the angelic nature of their own souls.

Angel Affirmation: Angels surround me during the darkest times of my life. They intervene when they can, but even when angels cannot prevent a tragedy they never abandon me.

Divine Timing—Spirit's Clock

You may want something to happen faster than it should. Why must you wait? Because of divine timing.

Some things you want will manifest for you very quickly—faster than you desire, even. That is because you are more ready than you know, or whatever is coming into your life is desperately needed there. At these moments your guardian angels will be with you to help you digest and manage the transition. Other times you may wait years for something you want that is indeed meant to be part of your soul's experience here on earth. You can try your hardest, pray your hardest, and still end up ... waiting. Your guardian angels are with you then too, giving you patience and wisdom and encouraging you to concentrate on the blessings you already enjoy.

Spirit and your guardian angels can see your life from what I like to call an angel's eye view. They see all your relationships, responsibilities, and growth opportunities in a way you never could. They can see the past, present, and future possibilities as well, and know when is the ideal time for an event to take place. When Spirit feels the divine timing is right, the angel realm will be able to help you manifest your dreams.

Have you ever wanted something desperately, had to wait for it, and because you had to wait you were able to make a better decision, get a better deal, meet a more appropriate person, or even change your mind completely? Has something ever happened faster than you felt ready for, but came along just in time to save you from disaster or promote you to the next level? You benefited from divine timing.

If divine timing has you in a holding pattern, your guardian angels can feel your current frustration. But they are sending you signs to slow down and accept this period of waiting. Work on surrendering the desire to control the timing of this situation. Take a break from this dream and count your other blessings. When the divine timing is right, your dreams will be given the "green light" as they say in Hollywood, or as the angels say in heaven—the white light, the blessing of Spirit.

If divine timing is bringing something into your life before you feel ready, your guardian angels sense your apprehension.

They are sending you confidence because Spirit knows you are more ready than you think. Angels are sending you guidance to help you navigate this new development. And they are sending you love to help nurture you through this transition.

> *Angel Prayer: Guardian angels, help me trust the divine timing of Spirit.*

ANGEL EXERCISE:
STRENGTHENING YOUR EMOTIONAL/ENERGETIC
BOUNDARY WITH HELP FROM THE ANGEL REALM

Earthly life exists on a physical and energetic level. The energetic level is largely unseen by the human eye, but it is just as present and substantial as the physical. The angels are showing me images and sounds of a loud city street: honking cars, yelling people, crying children, crowded sidewalks. The angels are telling me that just as you would want to block out these physical sights and sounds created by others that can be stressful and overpowering, so do you want to block out the emotions and energy created by others that can be overwhelming. Perhaps you walk into work and feel the collective stress of an office full of people on tight deadlines, and suddenly you are stressed too. Or maybe your spouse is dealing with long-term unemployment or health challenges and you slowly become as depressed as they are.

The energy and emotions of others don't just affect your own energy or mood—there are also physical consequences. The angels are showing me that just like getting punched in the stomach, negative or overpowering energy that you encounter can have an adverse effect on your body and your health. Remember, the energy and emotions of others that can overpower us doesn't always have to be negative. Intense joy, excitement, or focused determination can also make our hearts beat too fast or fry our nervous systems.

This exercise will enable your guardian angels, and probably some helper angels who specialize in emotional health, to create a stronger emotional/energetic boundary for you. Anytime you feel overwhelmed by the energy or emotions of others, perform this exercise. It will help strengthen your invisible energetic buffer, as well as remind you, on an intellectual level, that there is nothing to gain by taking on the energy and emotions of others. This is something that highly sensitive people need to be reminded of often, as it's so easy for these folks to tune in to the emotions of others and absorb the energy of a room. Feeling sympathy for others is noble and appropriate, but taking on their emotions or energy as your own doesn't help them—and it can only hurt you.

The angels are now showing me an image of someone plugging in to another person, as if that second person were an outlet. Then the angels show me the person who has been plugged into being drained—slumping over and shriveling up. This is a reminder that there are some people who will want you to take on their energy or emotion. They will try to plug into you like you're an outlet. Perhaps it feels comforting to these folks that they are not alone in their intense feelings or life challenges if someone else is mirroring their emotions and energy back to them. But the best way for you to help anyone is to stay strong and healthy and somewhat emotionally detached.

For this exercise you are simply required to relax and let the angels' divine healing skills take over. Energy is like Spirit: We can't see it, but it is one of the most powerful forces at play in our world. When you work with energy healing, you can make rapid and dramatic changes to your spiritual, physical, emotional, and intellectual self.

In a room where you can be alone, close the door, and block out noise, get in a comfortable position, either seated on the floor or lying down on a bed or couch. Address the angels out loud, in a soft, calm voice: "Angels, I need your help strengthening my emotional/energetic boundary. Please create a protective barrier around me now and always, that will guard against the emotions and energy I absorb simply by being in the world— the fear and pain I see on the news, the anxiety and urgency of my bosses and coworkers, the chaotic energy of crowds I walk or drive through, the intense highs and lows of my family and friends. Let the emotions and energy of family and friends seep in through this protective barrier only as much as is necessary for me to understand their problems and help, comfort them in their grief, or celebrate their victories. Let this protective barrier block me from absorbing the emotions and energy of my family, friends, and clients to the extent that their emotions overwhelm me, or that I take on their emotions as my own. I know taking on the emotions of others does not serve me or my loved ones. I know that being grounded in my own emotions and energy field is the best way for me to aid my family and friends, do the work Spirit brought me here for, and walk through the world. When I absorb the energy and emotions of others I am no longer in tune with my own energy or emotional needs. Let this angelic protective barrier you create or strengthen today make me feel more centered in my own emotions and soul."

Now imagine several angels around you. They have beautiful feather wings and flowing garments. They open their mouths and blow a white, foggy substance from their lips. Slowly this ethereal mist builds up and surrounds you on all sides. There is enough room for you to exist comfortably within the cloudy walls of this angelic mist. You can see the world outside, and this mist is permeable enough to let some things pass through. You feel safe and at peace here within this angelic chamber.

Close your eyes and meditate for five minutes, or longer if you choose, on these images of angels building a protective emotional/energetic boundary around you, and your feelings of peace, safety, and grounding inside it.

When you open your eyes thank the angel realm for helping you build this emotional/energetic boundary. This boundary will be with you always, but know that anytime you feel overwhelmed by the emotions or energy of others, you can close your eyes and picture your guardian angels strengthening your emotional/energetic boundary with their sweet, gossamer breath.

The angels are guiding me to tell you that if you ever again feel the emotions or energy of others making you frazzled, take stock of your emotional/energetic boundary. The angels are showing me a picture of a piece of cloth that has holes in it, like Swiss cheese. At any time, you can close your eyes and picture the current state of your emotional/energetic boundary. Is it healthy—sturdy, smooth walls of cloudy mist? Or are there patches and holes in the boundary where it has been worn down lately? If it's looking like Swiss cheese, think back over recent events and see if you can locate some situations or people that may have drained you more than you realize. You might need to take a little break from these situations or people, and also do some self-care. Don't forget to ask the angels to do a little repair work on that emotional/energetic boundary too!

Angel Exercise:

Ask Archangel Michael to Cut Energetic Cords

Along with your physical body, you also have an energetic body. And just as you do regular maintenance on your physical body (get a massage, complete a spring detox, have your hair cut) you need to also perform regular maintenance on your energetic body. An excellent way to keep your energetic body light and vibrant and healthy is with cord cutting.

Energetic cords are energy bonds that connect you to another person, much like an umbilical cord connects a mother to a child. These cords are invisible but they are very real. A cord can stretch through time (maybe you still have a cord to someone you haven't spoken with in years) and space (you can have a strong energetic cord that runs between you and someone on the other side of the world or in heaven). You probably share energetic cords with anyone you have an emotional relationship to—coworkers, family, friends, and even people you don't get along with at all. You can also have energetic cords to organizations or groups, like a company you work or volunteer for, a church you attend, or a neighborhood you live in. Normally these cords aren't a problem—it simply means these folks or groups are part of your life and you care about them. But what about people you don't like, or groups you want to move on from? Those don't sound like fun cords! Or what if you do like someone, but you can't stop thinking about them and it feels smothering or unhealthy? Or what if you love someone dearly but you had a big fight with them recently and can't seem to move past it? Or what if you can't seem to get over a relationship with someone or an organization that ended long ago? These are all scenarios when you may have an energetic cord that needs to be cut.

Sometimes cutting an energetic cord between you and another person will help you end a relationship you need to get out of. Or sometimes it will help you keep the relationship, and simply start fresh—enabling you to get over a recent fight or unhealthy pattern. Or cutting cords can help you forgive someone for a past wound they inflicted on you or help you move on from that person and that wound to a new level of healing.

We can also have cords to ideas and places. Maybe part of you longs for adventure and change, yet you are having trouble moving away from the town you grew up in. Perhaps a ceremony cutting the cord between you and your hometown will help. Or maybe you have an old idea of yourself as always being poor, or always struggling with your weight, and cutting the cord to that idea might help shift this pattern for you.

Whatever kind of cord you need to cut and whatever your reason for severing it, Archangel Michael can help. Because Archangel Michael is a divine protector who always carries a sword of light, this angel is perfect for the job.

For this exercise, go to a quiet room where you can be alone and shut the door. Think of the person, place, idea, pattern, situation, organization, or group that you feel you need to cut cords with. Tell Archangel Michael, out loud in a calm, soft voice, who or what you want to cut cords with. For example, you might say, "Archangel Michael, I'm asking you to come here today to help me cut any energetic cords I have to the idea of me living in poverty." Or, "Archangel Michael, I need your help today cutting cords between me and my old boyfriend." Or, "Archangel Michael, my dear friend and I got into a nasty fight. Can you help me cut the cord that represents this fight?"

At any point during this exercise, don't be alarmed if you feel a significant presence near you or feel the energy of the room shift. That is just Archangel Michael answering your call—if you are sensitive to energy you will definitely feel his significant presence!

Tell Archangel Michael a little bit about this cord, and why you want it cut. You might explain that you live modestly and work hard but are always struggling to pay your bills and don't have any savings. Or you might tell Archangel Michael that you and your ex-boyfriend broke up years ago, yet you still have angry thoughts about him regularly. Or you might explain the fight you had with your friend, and how you two are having trouble moving past it.

Next, tell Archangel Michael how you hope cutting the cord will help. Maybe you hope cutting any cords with poverty will help you get better at managing money, help you psychically break out of a cycle of poverty that has been part of your family's history for generations and may be subconsciously affecting your decisions around money, and encourage you to go back to school for a better-paying job. Maybe you hope cutting the cord between you and your ex will help you heal from the hurt that happened during the relationship and really work through your emotions, energetically help you attract a new partner, and enable you to trust potential new partners more. Maybe you hope cutting the cord that represents the fight you had with your friend will bring you two closer together, allow you to forgive each other, and help you respect each other's opinions and emotions more.

It might be helpful to close your eyes during this next section of the exercise. Just read one step, close your eyes and imagine it, and then open you eyes to move on to the next step.

1. Think of this person, place, idea, pattern, or situation you share a cord with, and imagine in your mind what the cord looks like. What color is the cord? What material is it made of? Is it thick (possibly indicating that the cord is very old or very strong) or is it thin and wispy (maybe this cord isn't too intense)? If you have trouble picturing the cord, imagine it as a golden, glowing rope.

2. Now get a mental image of the person, place, idea, pattern, or situation you share this cord with. Imagine that this cord is connected to both of you. See it starting at your stomach or heart and stretching to the person, place, idea, pattern, group, or situation you share it with.

3. Next, picture Archangel Michael with his enormous feather wings and mighty sword of light. He smiles very broadly at you, his eyes twinkling with kindness. His energy is protective but loving. You feel safe with him near. He nods at you to indicate that he is ready, then raises his sword, and in one quick movement severs the cord. It vanishes! Little bursts of colored light fill the space where the cord used to be. Archangel Michael gives you a hug, and then he flies off.

4. Now thank Archangel Michael aloud for helping you.

After this cord-cutting exercise, don't be surprised if you feel differently. Common reactions are: feeling drained or tired, feeling lighter, feeling giggly, feeling emotional, feeling sad, feeling sentimental, feeling peaceful. These feelings will fade as the day goes on. Remember, you must follow energetic work with work on the material level. If you want someone out of your life, don't take their calls. If you want to have more space in a romantic relationship, don't spend every spare second with your partner. If you want to move on from a painful relationship in your past, seek counseling or read a book on emotional healing. If you want to move away from where you are currently living, talk to a friend who made a big move, research new towns, or start by taking a small trip.

The energy work you've done today will help facilitate the change you seek, but you have to follow through with other actions. If the cord between you and this person, place, idea, pattern, group, or situation is very old or very strong, you may need to perform this ceremony more than once. But wait a few weeks and rest for now. You did a lot of big work today, and change takes time!

3

———————●———————

How to Recognize
Angelic Guidance

The angels want to offer some clear and practical guidelines about how to recognize their guidance. Your relationship with your angels is special and unique, so always trust what resonates and feels true to you, but the following suggestions should help. You might find it's easier for you to get angelic guidance by one or two of the methods outlined here, much more so than the others. This is normal and will vary from individual to individual. As always, run anything you believe to be angelic guidance through your own filter of common sense and intuition. The more you work with angelic guidance—by looking out for it and acting upon it—the better you will become at communicating with your angels and the more guidance your angels will send. It should also be noted that all of the methods of receiving intuitive guidance outlined here are the same ways that Spirit, ascended masters, spirit guides, and your own higher self can send you guidance.

Hearing Angelic Guidance

Have you ever heard a voice in your head, and known it wasn't your own? When an angel, other spirit guide, ascended master, or even Spirit speaks and only you can hear it, the voice will feel disconnected from you, unlike one of your own thoughts or fears. This is sometimes referred to as clairaudience. These messages arrive quickly and fully formed, not like a thought of your own that takes a few seconds to develop or work through.

Often we think the same things over and over, and these messages from the angel realm will usually be unique ideas that come as a surprise. Perhaps the angels give you a solution to a persistent problem, a solution that you would not have arrived at on your own. The angels might reveal something about yourself, or your situation, that makes you feel comforted or confident or hopeful. Or, the angels might offer a warning that certain attitudes or actions are not appropriate or might even be dangerous.

Whatever the message, the angels will never deliver it in a way that feels scary. Even when their message is one of urgency or warning, it will be delivered in a calm, steady voice. (The exception to this being if you are crossing the street and about to be hit by a car. Then an angel might shout, "Look out!") It is worth mentioning here that there are some mental illnesses where people "hear voices," troubling voices that are not their own thoughts and feelings. This is not clairaudience or angelic communication. Angels will never tell you to hurt yourself or anyone else, and angelic voices will never feel tormenting, agitating, cruel, or distractingly constant.

Hearing your angels speak right into your inner ear can give you a wonderful sense of how close your angels are, and how closely they follow your thoughts, as much of what they say will be like a direct answer to your own thoughts.

Seeing Angelic Guidance

Sometimes we are given valuable information about our emotions or a situation in our life via an image that flashes through our mind. Again, this is one way the angels can send us messages, otherwise known as clairvoyance. One thing to always keep in mind if you are prone to getting angelic messages as pictures is that these images are sometimes a metaphor. Perhaps you've been looking back on your life, and wondering where Spirit was during your darkest hours. Suddenly you see a picture of yourself stranded in the middle of a stormy ocean. Yet you are holding on to a buoy, and able to safely float there in the middle of the sea. Your angels are trying to tell you that even though you have been through challenges, Spirit was always there, making sure you had what you needed to get through difficult times. Or perhaps you are embarking on a new business relationship, and an image flashes in your mind of your potential partner down on all fours, head bent to the ground, listening. The angels are telling you that one of your partner's biggest talents is being able to know what is happening in your industry, what will sell and what won't. She has her "ear to the ground." Other times the image will have a simple meaning: a mental picture of your car glove box when you are wondering where you left your lipstick. If these images aren't straightforward, it can be a fun game between you and your angels for your angels to send these visual puzzles and for you to try and interpret them.

Knowing Angelic Guidance

There are moments when we just know something, instantly. Most angelic communication comes quickly, or in a flash, but when the angels gift you with information that you suddenly just know, like a download from heaven, it happens faster than the blink of an eye. This is known as claircognizance.

Maybe you were watching a love scene in a movie, and a king informs his would-be queen that they must part, even though he loves her. As the camera zooms in for a close-up of the king as he delivers this message, in a flash you realize this is exactly how a former love felt about you: This person cared deeply for you, but felt strongly that a separation was to your mutual benefit, even though that decision was painful for your love to communicate—and painful for you to hear. Or perhaps you are simply lost on a car trip, and in the midst of the chaos and tension of those around you and your own anxious thoughts, you suddenly get a strong knowing about which way to go.

This method of angelic communication is useful because you don't have to sit with or process the information given to you, even if it is about a complex relationship or situation—you understand the message instantly. It's also a great way for angels to impart a lot of information to you quickly, handy for times like when you are giving a friend counsel and suddenly just the right words of insight or comfort or advice come out of your mouth. Or when you are working on a big project at a new job where you are inexperienced and all at once you understand how to solve a complex problem.

Feeling Angelic Guidance

Do you ever get a "gut" feeling about something? Possibly you met someone and felt an instant connection or "electric energy" move between the two of you, or just got a gut feeling that this person —doctor, boss, teacher, Realtor, romantic partner, friend—is supposed to be in your life. Or have you read something in an article and gotten the uncanny sense that it applied exactly to your situation? Were you ever told a miraculous story, and had the hair on your arms stand on end? Can you walk into a room and feel the collective stress—or joy—of the people there? Or maybe you get a gut feeling of warning and foreboding about certain people or places. Are you sometimes overwhelmed by the emotions of others, as if you can actually experience their pain or excitement? This is called clairsentience, and if you are naturally highly clairsentient you are very sensitive to energy, and can sometimes find being out in the world a bit much!

This method of angelic communication is very common, so keep an open mind the next time you have a hunch, good or bad, about a person or a situation. It might be the angels trying to lead you in the right direction or connect you to the right person, and save you valuable time and energy. Angels also use feeling messages to tell you about the needs of friends and family. You might get an uncontrollable impulse to pick up the phone and call a friend. You're not sure why, but you have a feeling she needs someone to talk to.

Numbers as Angelic Guidance

Angel expert Doreen Virtue often points out the significance of number sequences as angelic communication. The number 444 is the most common. Much like when Victorian ladies would visit a friend's house and leave their card with the butler if their acquaintance wasn't home as a sign that they had called, so do angels use the number 444 as a calling card to let you know they are nearby. Catching sight of a clock at 4:44, seeing a bill for $4.44, or being given an address or phone number that includes 444 are all ways the angels remind you of their presence. Seeing the number sequence 444 can be especially comforting when you are waiting for news about a big project, working toward a long-term goal, or just feeling down and lonely.

Angels are also very aware of numbers that are significant just to you, and will send you those numbers as messages. If you're favorite or lucky number is 21, and you're going on a job interview and discover that the company is on the 21st floor, it could be a sign from your angels that this is indeed the job for you! Or maybe just as a thought crosses your mind about how you should view a situation in your life, you happen to glance at the number 21 on a calendar. The angels might be telling you that your insights are right on!

Synchronicity as Angelic Guidance

Carl Jung, the famous psychiatrist and philosopher, defined synchronicity as a "meaningful coincidence." Perhaps you looked at your bank balance, thinking you really needed to take on some part-time work to make ends meet. That night an old colleague e-mails out of the blue and says he's so busy that he has a job he must turn away—would you like to take on the project?

Is this a random coincidence, or the kind of meaningful coincidence Carl Jung wrote about? Most likely it's full of meaning—the universe and your angels letting you know they have your back by sending exactly what you need. Synchronicities can be small things too, like when you are feeling hungry and someone offers you a snack, or when you're wishing for more fun and your mate comes home early from work and suggests a bike ride.

Ever have people mention the same movie, song, or book to you over and over? Your angels probably know there is a message for you in this piece of art that will resonate with significance right now. Ever keep running into the same person, even a stranger, over and over again? The angels have probably timed these meetings because this person, or simply their presence, contains a message for you. Maybe this is someone you are meant to meet or spend more time with. Or perhaps this neighbor or fellow commuter is someone you see whenever you aren't taking good care of yourself, or need to slow down, or are about to receive good news. When something or someone appears continually in your life, it's a given that Spirit and the angels are sending them your way for a reason, like a clue on a treasure map. It's not by chance—it's synchronicity. Unsure what the message is behind the synchronicity? Get quiet and ask your guardian angels to give you the answer, either in words, pictures, knowledge, or feelings.

Dreams as Angelic Guidance

One of the biggest obstacles to receiving or recognizing angelic guidance is our own mind. Sometimes our heads have so many thoughts swirling around that we might not have room or space to recognize angel messages. The more instances throughout the day when we can sneak in some quiet moments, and train our brains to be still, the more open we become to angelic guidance.

When we're asleep, it's much easier for angels to get inside our heads and offer guidance—and sometimes lots of it! Ask yourself the following questions to discern whether a dream was just something random or an important message from an angel, your higher self, etc. Do you have a strong, clear memory of the dream, even if you usually have no memories of your dreams or only foggy memories? Did the dream seem to end right before you woke up? Did the dream feel more real, or vivid to you, than your normal dreams? Does the dream feel significant to you, like there was a message in it you needed to hear? Did the dream give you practical information that your conscious mind was not aware of, like the specific name of a supplement, company, or person you have never heard of before? Did someone from the other side, like a loved one who passed, visit you in the dream? Did an angel visit you in your dream? Was there information about a specific future event in your dream? Answering yes to any of these questions might indicate that an angel was communicating with you while you slept.

Angel Oracle Cards as Angelic Guidance

Angel oracle cards have become increasingly popular in recent years, thanks to the many decks created by Doreen Virtue. They are yet another way to receive guidance from your angels. Angels love these cards, because angels are always excited about new ways to communicate with you. The concept is based on the tarot system, which no doubt angels have used to communicate with people in the past. Only these angel oracle cards are dedicated to angels and usually depict images of angels and archangels. Angels are honored by these images and, sure, get a kick out of being in the spotlight! The messages written on the cards are penned in the voice of an angel: loving, encouraging, and gentle—even when the cards also offer a warning or suggest you make changes.

Look at a few different angel oracle decks at your local bookstore or new age shop and see which deck calls to you. Most will have a book inside that explains each card and offers you tips about giving yourself and others a reading. But really all you need to do is ask the angels a question and draw a card, or simply draw a card with nothing special in mind to see what the angels most want you to know right now. Shuffle the cards, and when you get the feeling you should stop and draw one, do so. That feeling is an angel nudging you. I like to see which cards stick out or even fly out as I'm shuffling, and those are the cards I use for my reading. Whatever you do, don't get hung up on the process. You can't pick a wrong card—angels are always guiding your hands.

I started using tarot cards as a teenager and switched over to angel oracle cards many years ago. I personally prefer the angel oracle cards (if tarot or another type of card deck works better for you, that's great). I get amazing accuracy and insight through angel oracle cards when reading for myself and for others (go to tanyarichardson.com to book an Angel Reading with me). The cards are simple to use and interpret. No need to be intimidated by them! It really is fascinating how the angels make sure just the right card emerges at the right time. As with all other variations of angelic guidance, you'll get better at and more comfortable with angel oracle cards as you practice over time.

Family and Friends as Angelic Guidance

Spirit speaks to us through our loved ones, because that is one of the best and most direct ways to reach us. It's common for your angels to put an idea into the mind of one of your friends, knowing they will share the idea with you. Ever had a friend or family member tell you exactly what you needed to hear to feel comforted, courageous, hopeful, loved, or safe? Ever had a friend or family member give you the perfect advice? Say something that gave you chills? An angel probably urged them to make this communication. Of course sometimes friends and family can drive us crazy, and say exactly the *wrong* thing! Or they might give us well-meaning advice that just doesn't apply to our situation or doesn't ring true. But when a friend or family member says something that resonates deeply with you just when you need to hear it—pay close attention. This might really be a message from your angels!

Angel Prayer: Dear angels, assist me in recognizing and interpreting all the guidance and wisdom you send me on a regular basis.

Angels Communicate Through Music

Angels are music lovers, record geeks, and divine DJs. That's because music has the capacity to instantly change our emotions. The opening chords of a favorite song can bring you to tears or put a smile on your face—or possibly both—within seconds. And angels know how powerful and healthy it is for humans to be in touch with their emotions. Angels are also attracted to music because, like the world of Spirit, we can't see music or touch it. Like your guardian angels, music travels on the ether, permeating your senses and calling forth your soul.

So it's no wonder that your guardian angels love to communicate with you through music. Do you have a song that reminds you of a loved one who has passed? You probably hear it in stores or on the radio around your loved one's birthday, or whenever you miss them most. Is there a song that helps you get your confidence and fire back? No doubt the angels make sure you hear that song when you're feeling uncertain or defeated. For years I was learning how to treat and manage a chronic condition, and every time my illness was about to flair I would hear a song by one of my favorite hard rock bands. I always got a sinking feeling when this tune—which was not one of their hits that received regular radio play—came on the radio, but I was thankful for the heads-up from my guardian angels. They let me know it was time to visit my doctor and stick close to my supplement and diet regimen.

The angels also know that music is a potent healer, and they encourage you to turn to music as medicine whenever you're hurt or afraid. The songs of a favorite artist can instantly calm your nerves or give you courage. And music can help you get in touch with and express difficult emotions. Turn up a song that speaks to your broken heart and shout out the lyrics. Or use music to celebrate by cranking the tunes and dancing and prancing around your living room when you've won a major victory.

The angels encourage you to make a soundtrack of your life. Write down or take mental note of the songs that the angels have sent you over the years to comfort, inspire, or heal. If you hear a song that holds meaning for you when you need it most, or you seem to encounter a song often, it's a sign the angels are serenading you.

Make a playlist of songs that have the most meaning for you, or songs that were sent by your angels. Or make playlists of songs that are useful when you need emotional support—songs for courage, songs for hope, songs for peace of mind, songs for love, songs for rebellion, songs for celebration.

Angel Affirmation: Angels send me messages through music, and I am always listening for my guardian angels' guidance.

4

•

Honing Your Intuition to Receive More Angelic Guidance

Your intuition is the most common way you receive messages from your angels. It's also the most common way to receive messages from your soul or higher self, your spirit guides, loved ones who have passed on, and Spirit itself.

Intuition is something that every human posseses. Unfortunately most people rarely explore or hone their intuition, and without regular exercise this important muscle will atrophy. The following chapter gives you a chance to reflect upon and examine your own natural intuitive abilities and preferences, as well as offers you exercises to improve them.

Your Individual Intuitive Makeup

Intuition—or sixth sense—is something every human is born with, without exception. However, some people will naturally have a stronger sense of intuition than others, just like some people are natural athletes. Did you know a few kids growing up who seemed to be good at every sport they tried? Basketball, football, hockey, baseball, track, skateboarding, mountain climbing, tennis—sure, these kids probably didn't participate in all of those activities. But these natural athletes were picked first for every team, because the whole school knew that no matter the rules or the game or the equipment or even their lack of experience with a particular sport, these kids would be exceptional players.

Similarly, you probably knew kids in school who were natural musicians. Or natural scholars. Or natural artists. Or popular kids who were naturally good with people. By the time we reach adulthood, most of us figure out a few things we are just naturally good at (nurturing, organizing, humor, etc.). Some people will find it easy to get regular intuitive information from angels and the spirit world through a variety of ways: clairaudience, clairvoyance, clairsentience, claircognizance, dreams, etc.

I am *not* a natural athlete—as a child, my family bestowed upon me the sarcastic nickname Grace. I remember when I tried out for the basketball team in junior high. "You're so tall, Tanya," one of the coaches told me, "that I think you'd be a natural for basketball." I got excited, picturing myself racing up and down the court covered in sweat, scoring the winning points just as the final buzzer sounded. The coach was all smiles the day I came to try out. "Okay, just dribble the ball," she said. I did—pretty much.

"Now, don't look at it while you dribble." I couldn't dribble successfully without always sneaking a peek at the ball. "Try walking around while you dribble," the coach said wearily. Man, she might as well have asked me to sprout wings and fly to the moon. I showed up for practice for a few weeks, but didn't improve. Finally the coach told me that I was welcome to join the team, but I probably wouldn't get to play very often.

Track seemed safest—you didn't have to deal with a ball or interact with other players. I tried short distances, middle distances, long jumps, high jumps, hurdles. At last I found my event—long distance! I wasn't the best in my school, but I was second best. And when we went to meets I usually placed and earned a ribbon. I wasn't a natural athlete, but I could run long distance and hold my own. And I honestly loved running, as well as the camaraderie of being part of a team. Track also taught me how to push myself beyond my known limits—a lesson I still value.

You might be as naturally gifted at intuition as I am at sports. That doesn't mean you have no intuition, it just means you will have to practice a little harder to find your intuitive niche, or the best way you receive intuitive guidance. In other words you'll have to find your long-distance race. Maybe feeling or knowing or hearing or seeing guidance is easiest for you, or maybe even two of those feel natural. The best way to discover your intuitive niche is to play with several methods, and this chapter will help you get started.

If you're naturally very intuitive you've probably already figured this out about yourself. I figured it out as a child, when my brother and I started playing an intuition game when I was twelve and he was nine. My brother owned some flash cards that were solid colors. Each card was glossy and either a bright red, blue, yellow, or green. I'd seen a television documentary about a psychic institute where they tested an individual's psychic abilities with various exercises, and my brother and I came up with a game using his cards to test our intuition.

My brother would turn away from me and I would close my eyes. Then he would pick one of the cards and say, "What color card am I holding now?" I could always guess what color he was holding because that color would flash into my mind within a few seconds of his asking the question. It was uncanny how I could always guess the correct color and my brother and I were both struck by my accuracy. Once I remember being upset because I thought he'd stumped me—or that I was losing my intuitive ability. Several times in a row I could not guess the color of the card he was holding, because I kept seeing two colors in my mind every time he asked the question. "I don't know," I told him with my eyes closed. "I keep seeing two colors at once today. Right now I see green and yellow. I see both equally. I can't make a good guess."

"Oh my gosh!" my brother said. "I was trying to trick you so I have been holding two cards at once. That time I held both green and yellow at the same time!" My brother was only nine, but he had the emotional maturity to accept that what I was doing wasn't something weird or bad, but just a natural talent. He was very complimentary to me about this ability and made me feel like it was something cool. My brother could not guess the color of one of those cards to save his life (we tried a lot). However, my brother is a natural athlete. Watching him play football growing up was really a pleasure for me, because it's always fun to watch a person do something they do really well, and completely naturally. It is then that we are seeing their God-given talents, a glimpse of the divine. We can't all be good at everything. How boring would that be? Having a few things we do really well can give us clues about our soul purposes, and let's us contribute to the world by being of unique service to others.

If you are naturally highly intuitive, you probably have one method of receiving information that is dominant (for me this is clairaudience, hearing intuitive information like a voice in my mind). However, it should be relatively easy for you to improve your intuitive abilities in other areas with practice and intention. Only in the past few years have I started getting regular clairvoyant guidance (receiving mental images), and that relatively new skill is getting stronger by the day. I did not try to gain this skill, but as I focused more upon, trusted, and studied intuition, clairvoyance naturally came on line for me. Now that I have clairvoyance in my bag of tricks, I can honestly say I get regular intuitive guidance and information by all the methods outlined here. Highly intuitive people should avoid whichever way you usually receive information in the exercises below, and concentrate on another method to increase and balance your overall intuition. You'll enjoy the novelty of getting information in a new way!

If you aren't naturally highly intuitive, all the following exercises will be powerful for you. However, you should pick one method of receiving intuitive information and concentrate on that one for a while before moving on to another. As a way to practice honing your intuition, let your gut instinct guide you to the method you will concentrate on first. Which one sounds most interesting or exciting to you? Which one are you drawn to when you read through the exercises? That is the method that will probably come most naturally to you. Once you commit to trusting and utilizing your sixth sense, you will probably be amazed at just how intuitive you are!

Asking the angels for guidance doesn't usually work well when you ask for something specific or on a timetable (for example, asking to see a white feather this Saturday afternoon). So with each of these exercises below, it's best that you practice every day by simply staying open to receiving intuitive messages of all kinds at any time. It can be very powerful to start a journal that is entirely devoted to recording intuitive guidance you receive from your angels. This will increase your sense of commitment to these intuitive exercises and increase their sense of importance to you.

> *Angel Affirmation: Just like my soul, my intuitive abilities are unique. Everyone has a sixth sense, and with study and practice I can hone and increase my intuition.*

CLAIRAUDIENCE EXERCISE

Clairaudience means hearing intuitive messages. We all have voices in our heads, and often it's the ego talking. But there can be other voices too, voices that speak in calm tones and offer unexpected insight into our lives. This is one way the angels will contact you. You'll know you are getting intuitive information from the world of Spirit if the voice sounds like it is not your own, speaks in brief, concise sentences, and says something that doesn't feel like a thought you've had running around your head before. The information will be a surprise or remarkably insightful.

I had a fun clairaudient moment when I was preparing to shoot the author photo for this book. Jewelry is an obsession of mine, and I wanted just the right necklace to wear in my picture. I looked through my jewelry, picked out several necklaces, but could never decide on one. I knew it was silly to overthink it so much but I wanted to choose a necklace that would send the right message, one that captured the energy of the angel realm. Even if the picture was too small to really show the necklace, the right piece of jewelry would give me good energy for the photo, energy potential readers could feel when they looked at my picture.

Finally I gave up, and one evening while I was out of town for the weekend, I went for a walk. As I admired the brick buildings and cobblestone streets of the place I was visiting, in the dusk light I noticed a little boutique's pretty window display. *I'll just go look at their jewelry for fun*, I thought. Half-moon pendants, colorful crystal rings, bronze feather bracelets—this

was really my kind of jewelry! Just then Chrissie Hynde's song
"I'll Stand by You" started playing over the store's sound system.
I smiled—it's my personal guardian angel song, and I'd been
hearing it a lot since I started working on this book (see chapter
six to find your own guardian angel song). I started examining
each piece of jewelry closely and gasped when I saw a sweet gold
heart pendant with a little moonstone. The necklace automatically reminded me of my aunt Kristen. Kris collects hearts, and
her gentle, loving energy completely matches that of the angels. I
looked at my phone and realized it was almost seven o'clock. "I'm
sorry," I told the clerk, "are you about to close?"

"No," he said. "Keep looking. I'm just trying to figure out this
music. I want to change the station but the system won't let me."

I smiled. I knew who would not let him change the station!
My guardian angels. I left and told the clerk I might be back in
the morning for the heart necklace.

When I got back to my hotel I couldn't decide if I should
buy the little heart necklace or not. Then, as I was sitting on
the bed thinking it over, a voice in my head said, "It was made
for you." I remembered how my guardian angel song started
playing right after I walked in the shop. I thought it was just a
reminder from my angels that they were with me. *Had it really
been a sign about the necklace?* I thought. Then a voice in my
head said, "What more sign do you need?" I knew it was my
angels speaking, and I'm so glad I got the necklace, which I am
wearing in my author picture.

If you are good at public speaking or writing, are naturally chatty or articulate, or have a love for the written word and are an avid reader, you might lean toward clairaudience.

Every morning when you wake up, ask, "Dear guardian angels, please send me messages as thoughts spoken inside my head. Let these messages give me insight into my life, inspire me, and comfort me." As you move through your days, try to keep your mind still and quiet as much as possible. This will help you hear your angels better, as they won't be fighting to get a word in between your own thoughts—many of which are the same thought running over and over on a loop in your mind. Quieting your mind will help you recognize an angel's voice as it will stand out more.

At the end of each day, sit down for ten minutes and record any message you believe you heard from your angels in a journal. Keep doing this every day for a month, and at the end of each week make note of how this exercise is changing for you, any observations you've made, if you acted on any of this clairaudient guidance, which guidance was especially helpful, and if you are receiving more messages as the weeks go on.

Clairvoyance Exercise

This exercise will help you increase your ability to see angelic guidance. Angels can give you information in the form of pictures. These pictures can be straightforward, or they can be a metaphor. When I wrote the section of this book about fear (see chapter ten), I tried to think of a way to describe how angels are actually more present in our lives in times of crisis, and I got a flash of a firefighter grabbing equipment and racing down a pole. The angels told me, through pictures, that when we are terrified, it's like an alarm sounding in the angel realm, and all our angels go on red alert and kick into high gear. As you get more comfortable with images as angelic guidance, you will get better at interpreting the pictures angels send you.

If you are a visual person who enjoys art, film, photography, and design, if beauty and fashion are important to you, or if you are a visual artist or are good at drawing, you might naturally lean toward clairvoyance.

Every morning when you wake up, ask, "Dear angels, please give me insight into my life today through images. Let these images be fully formed and colorful and intriguing. Let them catch the attention of my mind's eye and help me understand their meaning."

Then every evening in your journal record any intuitive images you received that day. Explain them in words, but it can also be fun to draw them in your journal too—especially if you were blessed with the ability to draw well. (I'm a stick figure gal.) Record all the details and colors and people in these images. Spend some time jotting down a few theories about what the angels might be trying to communicate through this image, and then decide which theory resonates most with you. Repeat this exercise every day for a month. At the end of each week, evaluate how the images change. Are they getting more simple or complex? Are they in color or black and white? Do they come more often? Do they contain motion, like mini movies? Are you getting better at interpreting their meanings?

ANGEL EXERCISE:
RECEIVE DREAMS AS ANGELIC GUIDANCE

Angels can come to us while we sleep, and send dreams that act as premonitions, perhaps giving us a glimpse into the future of our career or romantic relationship. Angels can also give us powerful guidance through dreams, offering detailed information that our own minds could have never known. I once had an angelic guidance dream that was very simple—just the word "chromium" in big letters. I wasn't familiar with this word, and had to look it up online. Turns out it is a mineral that, in some folks, can help stabilize blood sugar, something I needed help with then. Yet another dream gave me information about a friend. She'd recently had a baby, and in my dream there was something seriously wrong with the child (in my waking life, to the best of my knowledge, the child was perfectly healthy). In the dream I kept telling my friend there was something very wrong with the child, but that it could be easily fixed if she just went to the doctor. "Take the baby to the hospital now," I told her in the dream. "They can help. But you must go—it's serious." In the dream it felt very urgent. When I woke up I was afraid to call my friend, a new mother, and tell her this information. I didn't want to frighten her unnecessarily. Even though I felt this dream was a premonition, I tried to convince myself that this was probably something that would happen in the future, when the child was older, and that I could share the dream with my friend when she was recovered from the delivery and was feeling more confident as a mom. After all, I'd spoken to her several times on the phone and the baby was fine. About two weeks later my friend called. "Turns out the baby was in serious trouble, but no one realized it," she told me. A quick trip to the hospital solved the problem, just as my dream predicted.

If you often have vivid dreams, often remember your dreams, have had dead loved ones visit you in dreams, have experienced premonition dreams, find it easy to get lost in daydreams, or have an active imagination, receiving angelic guidance through dreams might come naturally to you.

Every night before you go to bed, ask, "Dear angels, please send me intuitive guidance through my dreams. Help me remember these dreams when I wake up, and give me the courage to share these dreams with loved ones if I feel there is a message in the dream for them—even if the message may be hard for them to hear."

As soon as you wake up each morning, record any dreams you feel may have been guidance from your angels—this way you won't forget or alter any of the details over the course of the day. Guidance dreams will usually be ones you remember vividly, sense are very important, give you specific information, give you specific dates, offer insight into a loved ones' problems, give information that comes as a shock to you, or information you could not explain how you received other than via an angel.

Some Final Notes on Intuition

If you feel that something is angelic guidance, trust that feeling. The more you pay attention to and act on intuitive guidance, the more you will receive it. Again, always run any potential angelic guidance through your own common-sense filter and gut instincts. Intuition is a sense that every human possesses. Like a muscle, your intuition will increase and strengthen the more you exercise it, whether you are naturally intuitive or not. The better you take care of yourself (food, shelter, physical and emotional health) the better your intuition will become. If none of these exercises resonate with you, try playing with some of the other intuitive methods of receiving angelic guidance described in the previous chapter.

5

---●---

Back and Forth
Communication & Praying
with the Angels

Receiving messages from angels is one thing. But how about sending a message to an angel? Or even more exciting, back and forth communication with the angel realm. The angels are showing me an image of a red telephone—an old-fashioned landline. This used to be the symbol of a direct line, a phone that you could pick up and someone important was immediately available on the other end.

The angels want me to tell you that's exactly what it's like when you try and contact them. All you have to do is pick up the metaphorical phone (in other words: pray, journal, or send a thought to your angels), and an angel is waiting on the other end, ready to receive your message and, when appropriate, engage in a brief conversation with you.

There's no receptionist, no phone menu, no elevator music to endure while you are placed on hold. Angels always answer on the first ring! That said, there are some useful guidelines to keep in mind to achieve optimal communication with angels.

Sending a Message to the Angel Realm

The idea of talking to angels is an intimidating one for some, though the angels want to assure you that it needn't be. In fact, communicating with angels is actually easier than communicating with another human! That's because angels are always available to you. You don't have to hope they are home when you stop by for a visit or wait for them to read your e-mail.

You never have to plan out what you want to say to angels ahead of time. They aren't here to judge you, so you have nothing to hide. You don't have to play the diplomat with angels, or worry about their feelings or reactions to what you say—their love is unconditional. You never have to wonder if your angels will take you seriously, or understand what you are really trying to express, because angels are master communicators who can see right into your heart when you address them. They will never be angry or withdraw from you no matter what you tell them. You can be completely, brutally honest with angels. As with Spirit, you can even tell your guardian angels when you are disappointed with them or angry at them. Angelic communication is a safe place for you to express anything and everything. Isn't that a relief?

You can speak to the angel realm on any subject you wish, and you can also ask for almost anything: answers, wisdom, solutions, patience, miracles, peace, comfort, love, help. Sometimes you might want to pour out your heart to an angel, as you would to a trusted friend, not hoping for anything more specific than a loving ear.

You may also want to speak to angels simply to express gratitude for their presence, the blessings they have sent in the past, their guidance, and their unconditional love. Angels are just like humans in that they appreciate a simple thank you every so often.

Now that you know you can say anything to your angels at any time, there are still some useful guidelines to follow regarding the *most advantageous* times, places, and ways to send a message to the angel realm. Note that you can and will *receive* messages *from* the angel realm at any moment: while you are doing the dishes, while you are talking to your mate, while you are asleep. The following are merely guidelines for sending a message *to* the angel realm.

Angel Affirmation: Angels are always available to me, always happy to listen, and never judge me for what I express to them.

Ideal Times to Speak with Angels

Like a parent whose hearing is trained for the slightest noise or stirring from an infant, the angel realm is always listening and anticipating communications from you. But both in the early evening and early morning, the veil between this world and the next becomes thinner. Take a walk outdoors as the sun is either rising or setting, and you will no doubt feel this subtle, temporary shift, when the realm of Spirit feels closer, more immediate than usual. These early evening and early morning hours, especially outside near nature, can be an ideal time to commune with angels.

It is recommended that you address your angels when you are in a calm, open state of mind, say when you are cleaning the house or taking a walk and your mind becomes quiet and meditative. Any time you are feeling peaceful you are less likely to cling to preconceived ideas and solutions about the situations in your life, and will be more ready to receive the guidance of your angels, guidance that might be unexpected or out-of-the-box. Of course you will also seek angelic help and wisdom in times of crisis or emotional upheaval, when it feels like you are screaming or begging for assistance rather than asking! This is to be expected. But overall, the calmer your nervous system is when you address your angels and the more peaceful your mind, the better you will be able to recognize, and be open to, answers from the angel realm.

Ideal Places to Speak with Angels

The most beneficial place to speak to your angels is a place that is quiet. Again, this is so you can have the peace to compose your thoughts and hear, sense, or—if you receive mental images from your angels—*see* your angels' responses. This quiet place where you commune with angels should also have a degree of privacy.

Either a room with a door you can shut or perhaps a park bench where you can sit alone with adequate space between you and those around you. Praying with other people is a potent practice. But when you are trying to have a two-way conversation with the angel realm, it is best done on your own, without the distraction of others or their energy. Sometimes you will send a message, a question, or a request to the angel realm and not receive an immediate reply, but other times you will—and you don't want distractions when those angelic communications are coming down the wire.

Talking to your angels in a peaceful setting in nature can be helpful, since most people feel closer to Spirit in nature. Likewise a place that you consider extremely beautiful can be a sacred spot to commune with angels, since beauty also makes us feel closer to Spirit. You might designate a special sanctuary for angelic communication in your house, such as a home altar. Or you might like to visit a holy place of worship to conduct angelic communication, such as a chapel or a cathedral. Anywhere that heightens your connection to Spirit is always an excellent place to address your angels.

Ideal Ways to Speak with Angels

How should you send the angel realm a message? The most common way is just through your thoughts. You can structure these thoughts by simply thinking, "Dear angels," at the beginning of your communication, and end with, "Thank you, angels, for listening," when your communication is finished. If you aren't sure which angel you want to speak with, simply addressing "angels" or "the angel realm," is fine. If you want to speak to your guardian angels, you can start with "Dear guardian angels," or even address them by name (see chapter one). If you want to address a helper angel, make sure you include their area of expertise: "Dear angel realm, I'm addressing this communication to a helper angel who specializes in emotional healing." And if you are addressing an archangel, definitely call upon them by name, as in, "Archangel Michael, I need your help." Be sure to give the angel realm some details about your situation and what you need. While the angels already know all the details, it's an important exercise in free will for you to lobby for what you want.

Other ways to send a message to the angel realm include journaling or speaking to them out loud (just as you might say a prayer to Spirit out loud). If you journal to your angels, you might find that they respond in your journal, much like automatic writing (letting your mind go blank and allowing Spirit, your higher self, or the angels to write through you). When your communication is completed, you may look back over your journal entry and see several ideas staring back at you that were not your own, or seem like fresh, new ideas or breakthrough "aha" moments. These could have been inspired by your angels.

If you find that your angels like to speak to you through images they place in your mind, you could always open communication by sending the angel realm a mental image that expresses your question or situation or desire. If you hope to conceive a child, for instance, picture yourself pregnant with a large belly. Then perhaps the angel realm will send you an image of the time of year this will occur: a dark, snowy winter afternoon or a bright, flowery spring morning, for example. Or you might be shown a month from a page of a calendar. Or you might see an image of yourself in a doctor's office, perhaps signaling that there are some fertility issues you need to address with a healthcare professional before you will be able to conceive.

The best way to send a message to the angel realm will vary from individual to individual, depending upon what feels most comfortable to you.

Having a Conversation with an Angel

Once you get used to directly sending messages, requests, and questions to the angel realm, you might find yourself in a lively exchange with the angels, where you are asking questions or voicing concerns and then immediately getting replies from the angel realm. These angelic responses can come via hearing your angels' voices, thoughts that appear in your mind that are not your own, images that flash into your mind, a gut instinct, or by the sudden understanding of a complex situation as if you are receiving a download from heaven.

It can be very exciting when this kind of back and forth between you and the angels occurs. Although usually this type of exchange between humans and angels is brief, or at least much briefer than a conversation between two humans over coffee or on the phone. The angels don't talk for very long, but what they say is very dense, filled with wisdom and insight. Think of the conversations between Luke Skywalker and Yoda as a reference point.

As stated before, sometimes you will send a message to the angel realm and answers will not immediately come. The important thing is that you participate in two-way communication by addressing your angels and sending them your messages. Their answers will come at the appropriate time, in the appropriate form. Just because you do not receive an immediate response does not mean the angel realm didn't hear you, or that the angels cannot help. Angels always hear you, they can always help, and an answer from the angel realm will always come—though sometimes it will come in a form that cannot be immediately communicated. The answer from your angels might come to you in a dream while you sleep, or in the form of a person or opportunity the angels send at a later date.

Your guardian angels want you to remember that there is no right way or wrong way to communicate with the angel realm. The more you practice sending messages to angels, the more comfortable you will get with the process, and the more you will settle into a routine and style of communicating with angels that works best for you.

Angel Affirmation: Sometimes talking to an angel will be like talking to a friend: I will ask a question and an angel will immediately respond. But even if an angel does not reply right away, the angels still receive and value all of my communications, and will always respond in their own time.

The Power of Prayer

Your guardian angels want you to take in this phrase for a few moments: the power of prayer. You don't need to be strong, healthy, rich, grateful, or popular to harness the power of prayer. Much like superheroes in comic books have special abilities, prayer is your supernatural power. Prayer enables you to address the heavens, to summon your angels. Prayer is your magic wand, and when you wield it you wield nothing less than the power to change the world.

Every prayer is heard, whether it is screamed in a moment of desperation, thought hurriedly in passing, or offered up with great reverence and ceremony. Prayer is your ability to exercise your free will here on earth. So much of your life is determined already, from the family you were born into to many of the challenges you will face to lots of the people who will be significant to you on your human journey. Prayer is one way *you* make edits to the screenplay of your life. It's your chance to write in a scene, or rewrite a scene—to influence the casting. Prayer is your opportunity to tell Spirit and the angels what you need help with, what you desire, what you dream of for a loved one, what you hope to change about the world, what you want to change about your life.

Every prayer is heard, and every prayer is also answered, although often not in the way we expect. Spirit and the angels see your life from a vantage point that allows them to help you in the most advantageous ways, and bring the people and opportunities into your life that will serve your highest good (and the highest good of everyone involved). We may pray for something that, without our knowing it, will drastically take us off our life path. Like praying to get into an early childhood teacher-training program when you're meant to be a full-time artist. Or praying to move to one city, when your soul mate lives in another. Or praying to become independently wealthy so you don't have to work, when your next job will provide the skills for you to realize your potential as a gifted healer. Spirit and your guardian angels hear the nugget of your prayer, the basic longing or need once all the details you've added in have been stripped away. They will work to bring you the opportunities and people that are your best next steps regarding this prayer. Your job is to then listen and watch for guidance and signs from your angels about your prayer—and to take action.

Your angels particularly want you to be aware of the power of prayer to influence the lives of those around you, even strangers. Praying for a country that has just experienced a natural disaster, praying for people living on the street, or even praying for someone who looks sad on the subway, are not only sacred acts of kindness and compassion, but powerful acts. Your energy of love and good will leaves your body when you pray over these situations, and travels through the world, influencing life in ways you will probably never know or even be able to guess at.

Test out different ways to pray: with others around the dinner or breakfast table. Alone or in a group at church. Silently while you get ready for work in the morning. In hushed whispers as you rock a baby to sleep at night. While you kneel or stand in front of an altar in your home. As you hold an angel figurine and imagine your prayer going straight to the ears of your guardian angels.

How you pray doesn't matter. It's only important that you *do* pray, that you accept Spirit's invitation to dance through this life together—as partners. You and Spirit are co-creators not only in your own life, but in influencing the lives of those around you and throughout the world.

Angel Prayer: Guardian angels, please help me to remember the importance and power of prayer, and inspire me to make prayer a routine and cherished part of my daily life.

Angel Exercise:
Pray for a Stranger

This exercise will help you develop more compassion and allow you to see each human as the angels see them: precious and worthy of unconditional mercy and love.

First, pick out a stranger to pray for. This can be someone you see regularly, like the teller at your local bank, or someone you only glimpsed in passing, like a man on the street begging for money. Maybe you have an idea about what this person needs, like the homeless man on the corner. Or maybe you don't have a clue about the desires of this stranger's heart, like the bank teller.

Your prayer for this person might be something specific, like, "Spirit, please bring love and shelter and food to that homeless man I saw today." Or your prayer could be more general, like, "I don't know what the teller at my local bank needs, but surely there is something she's praying for. Let the energy of this prayer speed her highest good along."

You can pick a different stranger to pray for now and again, and think of that person several times throughout the week. Just get a mental image of them, and think a concrete prayer in your mind, or say one out loud. Or you might simply send the stranger loving energy, or imagine yourself giving them a hug or a pat on the back. Sending positive energy to another person is a very practical gift. On some level they will feel that love, even if they don't know where it's coming from.

See if there are also any action steps you can take for this person in addition to your presents of prayer and good vibrations, like donating time or money or clothing to a local shelter. Make an extra effort to smile at your bank teller or thank her sincerely for her help. Angels get so excited when you put on a set of wings and go out to do angelic work in the world that they want you to imagine them doing back flips and spirit fingers, like divine cheerleaders, whenever you pray for strangers.

As you perform this praying for strangers exercise, you will notice that the people you pray for become quite dear to you. Even if they seemed angry or curt when you encountered them, as you picture them in your mind and send them loving energy, your heart will soften to them. You will also get a sense of personal satisfaction and joy after praying for a stranger. This is the same sense of joy and satisfaction that your guardian angels get when they help you! That is why this exercise brings you closer to your angels. Now you have a glimpse into what an angel's life is like.

Angel Exercise:
Start a Gratitude/Prayer Jar

This exercise will help you incorporate two of the most significant lessons your guardian angels want to emphasize: the power of prayer and the power of gratitude. Gratitude jars are something I first heard about from Elizabeth Gilbert, author of *Eat Pray Love* and *Big Magic*, who encourages her fans to write down what they are grateful for on slips of paper and collect them in a jar or bowl. When you're feeling down and need a lift, you can reach in the jar, pull out a slip of paper, and remember how many blessings you experience each day. Prayer bowls are something I've seen mothers blog about online. Anytime these mothers think of a person to pray for—a friend who needs a new job, a family member who needs healing, a stranger on the street who needs a home, or some need of their own—they write down the person's name and their need on a slip of paper and place it in the prayer bowl. Then at dinnertime one of the children at the table reaches into the prayer bowl, pulls out a slip of paper at random, and the entire family prays over the matter together. It's a wonderful way to teach children about prayer, and get the adults in the house in the habit of genuinely caring about the needs of others. I insist you also write down prayers for yourself, because the angels want us to understand it's just as important to tend to our own needs and learn to ask for what we want.

For this exercise you will need two stacks of paper, each a different color (I use pink for prayers, blue for gratitude); a pretty, medium-sized jar or bowl (I invested twenty dollars in a gorgeous purple glass bowl at one of my favorite boutiques, but a mason jar will do); and a pen. Anytime you hear of a person who needs a prayer (it can even be a stranger you encounter in a store or hear about on the news), write it down on the pink paper, fold it, and place it in your Gratitude/Prayer Jar. Anytime you think of something you are grateful for, write it down on the blue paper and place it in your Gratitude/Prayer Jar. Don't worry that you won't be able to come up with enough ideas to fill your Gratitude/Prayer Jar. In time this exercise will become a routine part of your daily life, and you might need to invest in a bigger jar! Sometimes simply walking by the jar will inspire you to write something down, which is why your Gratitude/Prayer Jar should be kept out in the open at all times, with slips of paper and a useable pen beside it.

Whether the exercise is for your benefit alone, or you involve other members of a household like roommates, partners, or children, your Gratitude/Prayer Jar will bring you closer to your angels. Feeling and expressing genuine gratitude has the ability to draw more blessings to you, and, just like humans, angels love to receive a thank you for all their hard work on your behalf. Praying for yourself and others activates your free will, and thus enables the angels to do more to aid both you and those you pray for. Gratitude and prayer are powerful spiritual tools that have the ability to change your life and the lives of those around you.

6

Bonding with and Creating a Closer Connection to the Angel Realm

Most people who are "into" angels want to feel closer to their angels. They want more guidance from their angels and they want to feel the presence of their angels in their day-to-day lives.

Your relationship with your angels is like any other relationship: It grows and deepens over time, and becomes stronger, more dynamic, and more complex the more you pay attention to it.

And like the best relationships, bonding with your angels should not usually feel like hard work, but more like fun. More like "play," the angels tell me. On that note, I hope you enjoy this next chapter, and I hope it brings you closer to your angels.

Angel Exercise:

Make an Angel Altar in Your Home

Having a sacred place in your home dedicated to angels can help remind you of their comforting presence, create a closer bond with your angels, and even increase communication between you and the angel realm.

Some of you might already have a home altar—a space in your house, apartment, or room—designated to Spirit. You might pray there, perform ceremonies and rituals there, or simply enjoy your altar as a subtle reminder of the Divine. If space allows, you can create a separate angel altar, or you can simply incorporate some angelic elements into your current home altar. (If you incorporate your angel altar into an already existing home altar, I suggest setting aside an area just for the angels.)

Your angel altar can be anywhere in your home. Out of respect to the angels I would only add that placing your altar in the bathroom on top of your toilet or near a grease stain in the garage might be inappropriate. Keeping your altar clean and free of major dust accumulation or cobwebs is also a respectful gesture. Whether you keep your altar neat and tidy is a personal preference. I am orderly by nature and like things in their place. However, I have a friend whose altar is a gorgeous mess, with things strewn all over. It's got a wild, fun, creative, relaxed energy.

If you want friends and family to have access to the altar, perhaps place it in a corner of your living room (tucked away or high enough that it will not be disturbed by pets or young children). On the mantel of a fireplace or hearth is a lovely spot for an angel altar. If your spirituality is something you consider private, the bedroom or your study can be the perfect place to set up your altar so it is out of the way. Someplace flat and sturdy where you can place a few objects is all that is really required.

Items you choose to place on your angel altar, or in the angel section of your existing home altar, should make you think specifically of angels. If you have a deck of angel oracle cards, pick one with an illustration of an angel and a message that speaks to you. Then set the card upright on your angel altar. Use a card that particularly resonates with you right now. Then in a few weeks or months, you can swap this card out for another one that you find especially inspiring at that moment in time. Since angel oracle cards are a popular way to communicate with angels, seeing an angel oracle card on your altar might inspire you to communicate with your angels more often.

Feathers usually remind people of angels, as some angels' wings are made of hundreds of feathers—I witnessed this firsthand when I saw an angel (see chapter one). The feathers on your angel altar don't have to be real, since hurting an animal would never honor an angel. But a nice synthetic feather or an image of a feather, can be a unique and meaningful addition to your angel altar since feathers actually make up an angel's most distinctive feature.

Angel figurines are another possibility for your altar. I have some figurines that were given to me and several that I purchased.

Is there a child in your life who made a drawing of an angel? Children have a close connection to the angels because they only recently came here from the world of Spirit, and many children will instinctively draw stick figures with wings without knowing these are angels or what to call the images. A drawing of an angel by a child you care about can be an absolutely precious addition to your angel altar. As long as their parents don't mind you discussing angels with a child in your life, you can even commission a child to draw an angel for your altar.

Do you own any angel jewelry? Perhaps a pendant of an angel or earrings in the shape of wings? When you are not wearing this jewelry you can always lay it on your altar to add some pretty angel vibes. Angels are sensitive to beauty and beauty is one of the ways we can draw closer to Spirit.

Whatever angel paraphernalia adorns your altar, your angel altar will soon become a sacred place where you can connect with Spirit's winged messengers. Not everyone in your house has to believe in angels or utilize this altar, but I do recommend informing everyone of its existence, and requiring that everyone in your home respect your right to display and decorate your angel altar.

You don't have to commune with your angels exclusively at your altar, but if you ever need to feel closer to them, are struggling with angelic communication, or just want to add a little extra oomph to an angelic request, your altar can be a wonderful tool, like a divining rod that harnesses angel energy. The act of creating an altar signals to your angels that you want them to play a larger role in your life. Simply seeing the angel images on your altar every time you pass it in your home will encourage you to make more regular contact with your angels by giving them prayer requests, and this will also increase their influence in your life and their ability to aid you.

Celebrate with the Angels

Angels believe that celebrating life's milestones and accomplishments is just as important as achieving them. Angels are noble, high-vibrational beings that are closely linked to Spirit, but they still love to party!

Your guardian angels want you to enjoy yourself, and more specifically they want you to mark those special moments that don't happen every day: birthdays, anniversaries, work projects that get the green light, graduations, new homes, sobriety milestones, fitness or other health and healing milestones. Celebrating these benchmarks means acknowledging the important relationships and projects your soul came here for. So celebrating is actually serious, sacred, important spiritual work.

The angels also want you to celebrate more often for purely selfish reasons. They want to party with you! When you raise a glass to toast yourself or a loved one, imagine the angels in heaven doing the same. When you dance around the room after a big win, take a moment to look up and imagine the angels dancing too. (Angels are excellent dancers—they've got all the moves. My angels love to break-dance.) Celebrating is an excellent way to acknowledge not just all you have accomplished, but all that your angels have accomplished in helping you with your goals and relationships. Celebrating is an opportunity to stop and thank the angel realm for all the hard work angels do behind the scenes every day.

Lastly, the angels want you to know that when you don't stop to acknowledge an accomplishment or milestone, you are sending your subconscious some very dangerous messages. Messages like: I don't deserve to celebrate. I don't deserve a present. I don't deserve a break. I didn't work hard enough to warrant a pat on the back. I didn't do a good job. What I accomplished isn't a big deal. This relationship isn't a big deal.

These are all punishing, self-sabotaging messages. Exactly the opposite of the messages your angels send you all day long. Messages from the angel realm include: You are loved. You are worthy. You are special. You've been through a lot. You've accomplished a lot. You're doing the best you can. You should be proud of yourself. You need to forgive yourself.

Your guardian angels love you so much that it actually hurts them to see you treat yourself shabbily. So if you want to make your guardian angels happy, celebrate, and when you do, be very, very good to yourself. The message from the angel realm on this is clear: celebrate, and celebrate often. The big wins and the little ones. The major milestones and all the mini achievements along the way.

Angel Affirmation: I deserve to celebrate every chance I get, and my angels love to celebrate with me.

Journaling Brings You Closer to Your Angels

Journaling can help you record your favorite memories, get more in touch with your emotions, and set goals for the future. But did you know journaling can also bring you closer to your guardian angels?

The thoughts that emerge in the pages of your journal are often not the same old notions that your brain regurgitates and dissects over and over. Journaling is like digging for buried treasure. The ideas and insights you get while journaling are jewels that come straight from the divine realm of Spirit, where the angels live, from that deeper part of yourself that is connected to Spirit and an eternal wisdom. This wisdom helps you see beyond the surface level of your life to unearth deeper truths, like the foundations of negative beliefs or self-sabotaging actions. When you journal, you mine for spiritual and psychological gold. If you're trying to understand the lesson behind a challenge you're facing, or get solutions to a persistent problem, say a quick prayer asking your guardian angels to be with you before you sit down to journal. Your guardian angels will help you discover the "aha" moments you're searching for, the deeper answers that can change your life.

The angels want you to take regular sabbaticals from this hectic modern world. Setting aside even fifteen minutes a day, or thirty minutes a week, to quietly journal gets you in the habit of consciously removing yourself from the hustle and bustle of life. There's a reason that those who devote their lives to spiritual pursuits and service spend a portion of every day removed from the world in quiet contemplation. Quiet contemplation brings you closer to Spirit. Daily or even weekly journaling gets you in the practice of adopting a silent, meditative state. There is a stillness and calmness that comes when you go inside and put pen to paper. And once you begin training your mind to be still, that stillness will last with you long after you close your journal. It is in this quiet, meditative state where we can most easily recognize the guidance of our guardian angels.

Your journal is an ideal place to communicate directly with the angel realm. Just as a prayer may be thought, spoken aloud, or even sung, so can a prayer be written down. Is there something weighing heavy on your heart? Share that burden with your guardian angels in the pages of your journal, and that burden will be halved. Is there someone you need help forgiving? Write to your angels in your journal and ask them to work on your heart. Is there someone you want forgiveness from? Ask your angels to work on their heart. Are you looking for a job or a partner? Let your angels know what you need by providing them with all the particulars in your journal. Or maybe your angels brought just the right person or opportunity into your life, and you want to say thank you. Write your angels a thank-you note in your journal—they will read every word and be grateful. Your journal is the perfect place to ask your angels for help, thank your angels for answered prayers, and seek patience and insight from your angels when a prayer is not answered.

Journaling can serve not only as a record of your life, but as a record of your faith. Jot down the moments when your faith grew to a new level because the angel realm pulled off a miracle in your life or the life of a loved one. Record the moments when you doubted Spirit and your guardian angels. Record the moments when your guardian angels sent you a special sign, or you received a sign from a loved one who has passed. Look back at old prayers that were answered by your angels beyond your wildest dreams, as well as some of the unanswered prayers that you might realize, in hindsight, weren't really in your best interest. (One of the ways your guardian angels actually protected you was by making sure those prayers were not answered.) There will also be prayers that were not answered which still cause you pain. Ask your angels to comfort you, and give you some insight about why this prayer was not answered. Or how about those prayers that were answered in unexpected ways, almost as if the angel realm was throwing you a surprise party just to see the look on your face, or remind you that life is an adventure. Old journals allow us to see our life from an angel's eye view, and map our spiritual growth.

Taking the time to connect with yourself and the angel realm, and express what is on your mind when you sit down to journal, will help you stay more present in your daily life. Journaling will ground you in the moment and get you in touch with your emotions and the events of day-to-day existence. Your guardian angels want you to savor your life, not rush through it. How can you learn all the lessons and feel all the joy your guardian angels send you if you are sleepwalking through your days? Journaling the contents of your heart and mind on a daily or weekly basis forces you to be aware of what is happening in your life. Then you can decide what is working, and what isn't, and ask your guardian angels to help you set goals and make changes.

Journaling can help you feel more grateful. Your guardian angels want you to recognize all the blessings in your life, even as they help you strive to do more and be more. Expressing gratitude to your angels by writing down your blessings will make you realize just how many blessings you experience every day. Gratitude not only makes you happier, it brings you closer to your guardian angels because you suddenly sense just how much your angels adore you—just how many special people and opportunities and precious moments are carried into your life on angel's wings every day. Seeing how many blessings you experience, written down in black and white, will inspire you to act as an angel to others. There are people who desperately need your assistance, whether it's donating money to a charity, donating some TLC to loved ones, or just donating a smile to a stranger on the street. Your guardian angels want you to follow in their flight pattern, and be of service to those around you. When the angel realm blesses your life, the angels are counting on your joy and gratitude spilling out to bless the world around you.

Anything you do for the first time can be intimidating, and starting a journal is no exception. Some people find the blank page daunting. Where do you begin? What exactly do you write about? How much should you write? For people unaccustomed to journaling, or for those who find journaling a challenge, guided journals are a wonderful solution. For those who are old hands at journaling, guided journals can be a nice way to mix it up with something fun and different. If you're enjoying this book, you might try *Heaven on Earth: A Guided Journal for Creating Your Own Divine Paradise*. It's the guided journal I wrote, and a perfect place to start or continue your journaling practice, with lots of journal prompts to get you speaking directly to Spirit and your angels.

Angel Prayer: Guardian angels, as I journal about my feelings and experiences, please send me wisdom, guidance, and comfort to help me better understand my own needs, worth, and journey here on earth.

Beauty Is Worship

When you see something so stunningly gorgeous that your heart skips a beat, you are seeing Spirit. Spirit speaks to you through the challenges in your life, but Spirit also speaks to you, and soothes you, through beauty. Beauty has a high vibrational energy that is close to that of Spirit, and beauty therefore recharges your own spirit so that you can do all the good work, face all the challenges, and feel all the joy your soul came here for.

A rust-colored sunset, lush fabric, jewelry made from the metals and stones of the earth, the dramatic plumage of a bird. All of these are Spirit and the angel realm trying to get your attention. Trying to get you to notice, and be alive to, the present moment with all its sensual pleasures. Spirit is just as prevalent in the beautiful simplicity of minimalism as it is in the overwhelming intensity of the elaborate and ornate.

Beauty isn't optional. The angels want you to know it is as necessary to your life as air and water—without beauty the physical body may survive, but the soul will wither. Spirit wants everyone to experience beauty, no matter what your financial circumstances, which is why there is so much beauty in nature. Beauty doesn't have to be expensive, but it does have to be part of your life if you want a closer connection to Spirit and the angel realm.

Your guardian angels want you to indulge in beauty. Make beauty a daily practice—a worship. It will energize your own spirit while bringing you closer to the Great Spirit that is part of us all.

Angel Prayer: Guardian angels, bring me closer to you by showing me ways to bring more beauty into my life.

Angel Exercise:
Take the 30-Day Beauty Challenge

You've been led to this page—whether you are reading the book from front to back or skipping around—because your guardian angels think you need more beauty in your life, and would benefit from a month of intense beauty therapy. Beauty makes you more present and alive in the moment, gives you pleasure, feeds your soul, and brings you closer to Spirit, as beauty is one of the ways Spirit reveals itself to us here on earth. The angels want you to access more of Spirit and your soul in your daily life, and that means accessing more beauty.

Every morning for the next thirty days, the angels want you to wake up and ask yourself and the universe, "How can I bring more beauty into my life today?" See what answers come, both from your own mind and as signs from your angels, and then act on these ideas. Every evening, before you go to sleep, silently or out loud say this prayer, "Thank you for all the beauty that was brought into my life today." Then look back on your day, savoring all the times you were struck by beauty. In your journal you might record both your morning insights about how to bring more beauty into your life, and your evening reflections on the beauty you witnessed. Whenever you crave more beauty in the future, you can thumb through the 30-Day Beauty Challenge section of your journal and get inspired! Don't worry if there are some days where you are more active with this exercise than others, or some days where you forget it all together. The angels want you to work on curbing any perfectionist tendencies with the exercises in this book, and instead celebrate every insight as a major success.

The following are suggestions from the angels on finding beauty: in the faces of the people you see each day; in walks through nature, whether you experience a whole forest or a single tree by the side of the road; in the jewelry you adorn your body with; in the clothes you dress yourself in; in the way you arrange your hair or wear your makeup; in the way you maintain and decorate your home and workspace; in the tiniest of details, like the colors and design of the coffee cup you drink from every day; and in the grandest manner, like the moon glowing softly in the cool night sky or the morning sun as it sizzles just above the horizon.

Do you need to spend money to bring more beauty into your life during this 30-Day Beauty Challenge? No. But it would be an excellent time to treat yourself to a few things you've been wanting to update in your wardrobe or around your home. You might find them on sale or look at these purchases as a priceless long-term investment not just in your happiness, but in your sanity. The monthly beauty challenge might involve you simply becoming more aware of, and attuned to, the beauty that already surrounds you. Or it might urge you to spend time trying out a new hairstyle instead of watching television, or going out of your comfort zone by trying a new style of dress instead of sticking to the same old fashion choices, or shopping the sales for some pretty new pillows for your couch.

Be sure to also take note of how the 30-Day Beauty Challenge makes you feel: more confident, more alive, more peaceful, more vibrant, and hopefully closer to Spirit and the angel realm.

Angel Exercise:
Dedicate a Song to Your Guardian Angels

Guardian angels care for you so much that it's hard to convey the depth of their feelings. And since their communication with you is often accomplished via signs and metaphors, or with short intuitive flashes or messages, it's an extra challenge for your guardian angels to share the sentiments in their hearts. Yet your guardian angels are desperate for you to know how much they adore you, for you to know that there are beings of light who love you unconditionally, who have dedicated their existence to guiding and protecting you.

Guardian angels receive an enormous sense of satisfaction from loving you and keeping you safe, because all creatures, including humans, get tremendous peace from living their divine purposes. That sense of satisfaction and contentment becomes much stronger in guardian angels when their relationship with you is interactive. It's always beneficial to both you and your guardian angels when your bond is strengthened by two-way communication. The following exercise, dedicating a song to your guardian angels, is an easy method for you to achieve that two-way communication and enhance the connection you already have with your guardian angels.

Try picking a song that makes you think of everything associated with guardian angels: unconditional love, mercy, comfort, protection, guidance, inspiration. Then dedicate that song to your guardian angels. This dedication can be done through prayer, writing in your journal, or a single conscious thought. If you are hurt or afraid, if you want to celebrate or express gratitude, or if you just want to feel closer to your guardian angels, you can listen to your angel dedication song and imagine your angels serenading you. Think of each lyric, each note, as a message straight from your angels' hearts to your heart.

I personally have a song that reminds me of my guardian angels' presence in my life, and you should feel free to use it for this exercise if the song resonates with you. The tune I dedicated to my guardian angels is "I'll Stand by You" by Chrissie Hynde.

When I imagine my angels singing "I'll Stand by You" to me, it brings to mind the fierce, determined aspect of my guardian angels' love. Like mama bears, my guardian angels will protect me, and watch over me, no matter how dark the path before me, no matter the challenges and danger I face. This song illustrates how my guardian angels forgive me instantly and totally, no matter what is weighing heavy on my conscious. This song encourages me to express all my emotions, even the negative, complicated, messy ones, and encourages me to share those emotions with my angels—to confess everything to them. Because angels are more like us than we realize. They feel the pain of our suffering, and they feel anger at the injustice in the world. This song reminds me that there is nothing I can do to alienate my angels, nothing I can do to make my angels abandon me. When I imagine my angels singing this ballad to me, I sense they would walk through any fire on my behalf.

Choose one or two songs to dedicate to your own guardian angels. When you imagine your angels singing one of these songs to you, you will probably cry or get chills. That means you've hit on a song your guardian angels love too, one that they agree expresses their angelic level of love and commitment, something that is hard for the human mind to comprehend, except maybe through the magic and emotion of music, the language of angels.

Don't be surprised if you start hearing this song often on the radio or in stores—it's just your guardian angels reminding you of their presence. And feel free to play it whenever you need comfort, crave reassurance, or simply want to celebrate a victory you know your guardian angels had a hand in. When you listen to this song, know that your guardian angels are right beside you, giving you an angel-sized hug, offering your soul a soothing lullaby.

7

•

Angels & Nature

Angels delight in nature as much as humans do. The angel realm is showing me an image of angels flying through a forest with their eyes wide and their mouths open in wonder. Angels want me to share with you that they are also awed and humbled by the beauty of planet Earth.

The angels also show me an image of them solemnly laying their hands on plants and trees, sending their healing energy into every manifestation of nature. That's because the angels are committed to protecting and nourishing nature, just as angels are committed to protecting and nourishing humans.

When you are in nature, touched by its magnificence, moved to recognize it as a magical extension of Spirit, and motivated to defend and honor it, you are very close to the angels.

Angel Exercise:
Swear an Angel Oath to the Earth

The angels have a clear message for us regarding our current environmental crisis: Do not lose hope. But then angels never lose hope! They can always see the best-case scenario as a real possibility in any situation. And the angels want me to tell you these exact words regarding hope: "Hope can move mountains." Think about that popular phrase for a minute. Picture a mountain. To move one would truly be a miracle. Yet miracles are not wishful thinking. Miracles are "very much," the angels tell me, a reality.

Angels are forever guiding humans toward the best-possible outcome in any set of circumstances, and the angels are trying now to usher us into a new age where the earth is honored by every human inhabitant. An age where humans feel true humility before the forests and the oceans, and each human makes a commitment of service to this land.

Native American cultures understood that Spirit and the earth cannot be separated, and felt that being in nature was akin to being in a temple. So many of the daily practical tasks these cultures performed were done with ceremony and reverence. When they took from the earth, simply to eat, there was great meaning for these cultures in that act.

The word *humility* comes up often when angels express how they want humans to feel toward this planet. Angels never wish you to punish or unnecessarily deny yourself, but angels do want humans to sense that they are one small part of a whole, and that if we are going to save this paradise Spirit shared with us, then each human is going to have to make sacrifices. The angels explain that if the planet is to survive, we will have to look at the world in a new way, and approach our daily lives differently. This is similar to past enlightenments, such as the discovery of microscopic particles and the Civil Rights Movement. The angels are already busy giving ideas to inventors and businesspeople and individual citizens to help usher in these new techniques and ways of managing and viewing our daily routines. Just as one of the inventors of the atomic bomb later regretted his creation, so too does John Sylvan, the inventor of K-Cups, wish he'd never had the idea—or shared it.[2] Although Keurig says it is working on a fully recyclable K-Cup, the number of K-Cups sold in 2014 alone would circle the earth an estimated 10.5 times, according to *The Atlantic* magazine. The majority of K-Cups end up in landfills. Sylvan now runs a solar-panel company—the angels bow to him.

It can be discouraging to read news reports on people who don't care about pollution, people who are not recycling, people who squander precious resources, people who do not realize or accept how dire the situation is. For the situation is dire— angels will never lie or sugarcoat something for you, because ultimately that does not serve you. Angels *will* give you information in the most gentle, merciful, and accurate way possible. And the angels are always on hand to help, and will move heaven and earth for a worthy cause. The angels want to remind you not to get discouraged when you see others disrespecting the

---

2 "A Brewing Problem," *The Atlantic*, March 2, 2015

earth (often these people know not what they do). The most powerful thing you can ever do is change yourself. Do the right thing by the earth, in as many ways as you can. Always be open to new methods for protecting the earth, and educate others.

The angels would like us all to swear an oath to the earth, an oath to protect the earth from harm and nourish it with love. Let's take a page from Native American culture, and perform this oath with a bit of ceremony and reverence.

Go outside on a windy day (the wind is an exceptional way to physically experience Spirit's presence) and find a spot where you can have a bit of privacy. Kneel down and put your hand to the ground (this "ground" should be earth—soil or grass, not concrete). Feel the air hitting your face. Watch the leaves flutter in the trees, watch the stems of the flowers bend. With your hand still lying on the earth, say these words softly into the wind, "I pledge to be a good custodian of this magnificent planet Spirit has shared with me, and always look for new methods of stewardship. I will act as an angel to the earth. I will strive to follow the guidance of my angels, which will lead me to ideas for healing and preserving this planet. I offer this oath here and now, and will carry it in my heart forever."

ANGEL EXERCISE:
GROUND YOURSELF IN THE ENERGY OF NATURE

Angels know that everything in nature is holy, part of Spirit. People, animals, rocks, trees—they are all divine, because they all share that magical spark of energy that is the calling card of Spirit. The energy of things that were not created by man.

You can receive enormous amounts of healing from nature. You already sense this when you stop to watch a sunset and become mesmerized by the striking, transitory colors in the sky. After you witness the sun sneak behind the horizon, you probably feel more peaceful, more centered, and closer to Spirit. Likewise when you hold or stare at a crystal, you can feel an intense, clean, clear energy that has the power to transform and reset your own energy or that of a room.

This exercise teaches you to connect with the healing energy of nature more consciously. Once you get the hang of it you'll find yourself doing this exercise automatically whenever you're relaxing outdoors. The immediate benefits of this exercise are sensations of peace and grounding (being grounded means you feel calm, safe, and confident in your own skin and walking around in the world). If you are experiencing anxiety or stress, if you're facing a big challenge, or if you have survival fears because of illness or unemployment, this exercise can be done daily to help you regain your emotional and spiritual equilibrium.

The long-term benefit of this exercise is that it brings you closer to the angels, because this exercise will enable you to develop a deeper relationship with nature. Soon you will view even the tiniest elements of nature as the angels do: as breathtaking miracles. The angels see every part of this earth and its inhabitants as sacred. The more you adopt that same philosophy, the more in harmony and aligned you will be with the angel realm. In practical terms, that means more communication with your angels and a greater awareness of their presence and potential in your life.

Find a spot in nature where you can either go on a leisurely stroll or just sit and admire the landscape (I prefer to do this exercise walking slowly, but it's not necessary). As you walk, or as you look about from your seated position, slowly begin focusing on the details of the scene. The bark of a tree trunk, the shades of green in the grass, the path of a butterfly. Keep looking around closely, almost like you're a private investigator searching for clues. Soon you will be lost in this world of nature and its details. Your mind quiets. Time seems to stand still, as if you are opening a portal, a gateway to something eternal.

Now, don't just look at the plants and animals and sky around you, but start to *feel* them. Focus in on the petals of one flower and feel the energy coming off those petals. This energy is palpable, alive. Let the energy of the petals meet your own. Take it in and savor it for a few seconds. If you wish, you can smile at the flower, or silently tell it thank you before moving on to observe something else.

Pay very special attention to trees. Trees are mighty creatures with enormous energy. You will sense much coming from a tree, especially the big ones that have been around for a while. These trees have seen it all, and somehow you get the sense that they know it all too—they just choose not to say anything! The angels have hinted to me that these old trees are also angry because humans don't respect trees as much as we should in this culture, and so often we waste the precious resources trees provide. In fact, many trees feel *rage* about this state of affairs. But don't let an older tree scare you if you sense an aloof energy from it. Most trees will warm up to people, especially if there is a tree you regularly pass on a walk or a tree you like to sit beneath. Just doing this energy exercise with a tree, where you acknowledge how much they have to give and thank them for their healing energy, shows trees the respect they crave and deserve.

Note the differences in energy in different parts of nature. Maybe the petals of the flower have a light, playful, outgoing energy, and the trees have the energy of a wise elder. Also note how your own energy changes as you sit and observe the nature around you or walk through it. Does your heart rate slow down a bit? Do you catch yourself smiling at something you see? Do you feel more relaxed? At the end of the exercise you should feel calmer, safer, closer to Spirit, and more confident of your place in this world and your ability to handle, with the help of Spirit, any challenges you are currently facing.

People always associate fairies with nature, but angels are nature lovers too. Ask your guardian angels for help with this exercise if you need some inspiration. No one is better at energy work than angels!

Winter Is a Sacred Time to Commune with the Angel Realm

The angels want to remind you of all the opportunities you have for spiritual growth, and the dead of winter—after the holidays have passed and before spring distracts us with showy displays of color and warmth—is one of the most sacred times of the year. Winter signals stillness on the streets, a natural inclination to stay indoors, an overall sense of forced isolation that can, if harnessed, be a blessing. This invitation to turn inward is a chance to do the soulful work that can more easily be put off during busier months.

Consulting with the angel realm as you set intentions for the New Year, spending time in prayer and meditation, journaling, attending workshops, or reading books that will contribute to your personal growth, and experiencing the silent, white, holy quality of nature during the stark January, February, and March months sets the stage for a spiritual winter retreat. The space left empty where relatives and celebrations and end-of-year deadlines dwelled will now be taken up by the grandeur and weight of your own soul, and by the tangible presence of the angels and Spirit itself in your life.

The trees' bare branches remind us that winter is time to let go of relationships, attitudes, and roles that no longer serve us. Reflecting upon and releasing these things now allows something new and pretty and fresh to grow in their place come spring. Yet to consciously take an inventory of our lives requires us to embrace this time of solitude. Like the rollicking river freezes over and becomes still, so must we forgo activity and become still.

If the personification of spring is a mischievous fairy, ready to dance and sing and play in the sun with those of her kind, then winter must be a queen: reserved, noble, a keeper of her own counsel who has significant matters on her mind. A woman of mediation and strategy, who pauses to make sense of her past, analyze her present course, and plan her future. A woman who knows her company is as sought after and prized as anyone in the land. A woman who knows that after a busy season of parties and guests, it is necessary to retire to her chamber and tend to her own needs, her own thoughts, the whispers of her own heart and soul.

The angels will be right beside you as you perform your wintertime work of self-care and reflection. Guardian angels will give you insights about your past and your future, and send you love so that you do not feel alone in the isolation of winter, but closer to Spirit than ever.

Angel Affirmation: Winter is not a time to be dreaded, but a time to anticipate eagerly. A time of rest and rejuvenation for my soul, a sacred time to grow even closer to myself and to Spirit.

Imitate the Peacock and Put Your Natural Gifts on Display

Angels have a special relationship with any animal bearing wings. One reason is because these animals are the only ones on earth who have an inkling of the freedom angels feel when they take to the sky. Angels can move infinitely quicker than any earthly animal with wings, because usually angels are traveling between dimensions, not using their wings at all. But angels have been known to appear to people as flying or hovering or floating in the sky, as a bird might. Birds of a feather, or creatures of a wing, you might say! Also angels know that many humans associate animals possessing wings with angels, even if only subconsciously. Therefore your guardian angels will use these winged creatures, such as birds and even insects such as butterflies, to send you messages.

For example, when you find yourself confronted by peacocks: on T-shirts, in nature, or on television, or if you are drawn to peacocks and seek them out by purchasing greeting cards or art that depicts their image, your guardian angels might be hinting that you should take more pride in your natural abilities. These abilities were gifts from Spirit specifically designed to enable you to help others and fulfill your life's purpose. Therefore these abilities were meant to be on display, not hidden away.

The image of the peacock is a perfect way for the angel realm to remind you to show off your natural talents. If you've ever seen a peacock in the wild, you know they take extreme pride in their long, delicate, colorful, iridescent feathers, fanning out their trains to stretch several feet into the air, crowning their comparatively tiny bodies in a breathtaking display of beauty. The peacock is in touch with its natural gifts—its unique feathers—and makes good use of them. The peacock knows that displaying beauty to the world will give those around them great pleasure.

What were the gifts that you were born with? Maybe you are naturally good at nurturing, teaching, painting, finance, compassion, humor, healing, leadership, or music. We were all born with many gifts. No human is an exception to that statement. If several of your abilities don't instantly jump to mind right now, spend some time asking your guardian angels to help you identify those natural talents you were born with. Did someone make you believe that your gifts should be downplayed, or even hidden? Did someone during your childhood, or at your job, try to convince you that you weren't good at something—when you knew in your heart they were wrong?

There is nothing rude or selfish about assuming center stage in your life, and owning your talents and worth. In our culture there is a heavy emphasis on shame, something we inherited from older Puritanical belief systems that are hugely outdated. However, this Puritanical notion of virtue in extreme humility, to the point of shame at any show of pride, might still be operating in your subconscious mind. Do you resent your favorite musician when they walk out onto the stage in an elaborate outfit and play a solo that makes you wonder how anyone is capable of such genius? Do you shame the ER nurse who reacts instinctively to complex traumatic situations, has the ability to resist emotional reactions to extreme stimulus, and helps stabilize a patient who otherwise would have died? Do you deny the value of the father who is on-call 24 hours a day, who keeps children and a partner fed, supported, and loved, and acts as the foundation that allows his family to go out into the world and be their best? These people have talents they have honed over time with experience and hard work. They offer up precious, priceless gifts to our society, and inspire others to greatness simply by their example. What is the point in pretending these folks aren't excellent at their jobs? Or demanding they demur when negotiating a raise, time off, or more support? That serves no one—including you.

When you bury your Spirit-given gifts by denying and downplaying them, you cast a shadow over the light of your soul, the light you were meant to bring into the world. Get out there and strut your stuff like the peacock! The peacock knows its worth: a universal symbol of beauty and pride. Your guardian angels know their worth, and they want you to know yours too. You are so important that your angels, these powerful beings of light and love that are closely linked to Spirit, devote their entire existence to guiding and protecting you. That's because you have big talents, and big things you are meant to accomplish here on earth. Claim and nurture those talents, and you claim your power and bless the world.

Angel Prayer: Dear guardian angels, please help me identify those abilities given to me by Spirit, and help me to know my own worth, just as the peacock does. Give me the opportunities to hone these talents and share them with the world.

Butterflies as Symbols of Transformation

Another winged animal the angels will often send as a messenger is the butterfly. The butterfly's fascinating and dramatic metamorphosis from caterpillar to colorful, flitting creature is a universal symbol of transformation. Transformation is a popular theme with guardian angels, because helping us through the many transformations we undergo during a lifetime, and encouraging us to make as many metamorphoses as possible during our journey on earth, is a chief task of the guardian angel.

Often angels will send a butterfly simply as a mile marker to let you know you are in the process of a major transformation in some area of your life. The message from your angels when you encounter a butterfly in a story, on a T-shirt, or flying near you—or probably all of the above in a succession of synchronicities over the course of a few days or weeks—is to keep going. Have faith and courage regarding whatever you are experiencing—the end result will be as beautiful and unique as a butterfly. Major transitions can be difficult, messy, and painful at points in the process, but the angels affirm that you will be as surprised and delighted as that fuzzy little caterpillar with the outcome. The sign of a butterfly from your guardian angels also lets you know that what you are going through right now is a big, dramatic change. Have patience with the process and nurture yourself along the way.

We were each meant to experience a series of transformations during our lifetime. Most of these transformations are slow and gradual, and then comes a moment when it all starts to speed up and get more intense. It's then that we stop to spin a cocoon. Just like a healing crisis, it feels like a transformational crisis. Guardian angels are experts at helping us with these boiling-point moments, when we birth a new version of ourselves, reveal a new layer of our soul. The more we embrace these transformations, the more we can live at our highest potential. If you have difficulty with change, or are facing a big change that feels particularly scary, know that your guardian angels are closer than ever. Acting as midwife to you during this time is one of a guardian angel's main assignments. Watch for guidance from your guardian angels, ask for their help, and accept the comfort of their presence. Big changes can be an ideal opportunity to develop a deeper relationship with Spirit and your angels. You can use the image of the butterfly yourself as inspiration during a transformational period—by posting a picture of one in your home or at work—to remind you that your angels are ever present and helpful now.

Another occasion your guardian angels will send you butterflies as messengers is when a loved one has passed. Death is yet one more major transformation for the soul. If a loved one has recently passed, the angels may send you butterflies to let you know your loved one is in a place where they are happy and busy now, just as the butterfly always seems to be busily flitting from flower to flower, enjoying her new wings. So too is your loved one engaged and enjoying their new life in heaven.

If your loved one passed some time ago, but you have been missing them lately, your guardian angels might send butterflies to remind you that your loved one's soul is still alive. Your separation is only temporary, and at some point you too will spin a cocoon and emerge in heaven, where your loved one is waiting.

Angel Prayer: Guardian angels, please send me butterflies to let me know when I am heading into a major transformation, and surround me with butterflies when I am missing a loved who has passed on.

Embody the Dove and
Be an Emissary of Peace

The dove has more in common with angels than just its white-feathered wings. Like angels, the dove is a symbol of Spirit in many religions. In the Bible, the Holy Spirit is often described as descending to earth in the form of a dove. Many ancient goddesses, including Ishtar, Venus, and Aphrodite, are depicted with doves. And legend has it that onlookers saw a dove fly away from the stake when Joan of Arc was burned and killed for revealing that she had spoken with Archangel Michael. Today we usually associate the dove with gentleness, grace, and peace. These are also cardinal character traits of the angels, so you can be sure that if you're encountering doves—in nature, on television, or in art—you are being given a sign from your guardian angels that you would do well to embody the peaceful, graceful, gentle essence of the dove.

You might evoke the spirit of the dove if you are involved in a dispute with loved ones or coworkers, and you need to ground yourself in your inner diplomat. Before addressing an individual or a group that you have major differences with, ask your guardian angels to help you picture a dove, and infuse your talk or speech with the same gentleness and grace we have come to associate with this animal.

Or perhaps there is a conflict situation you are praying over that is so dire and extreme—like when two family members become estranged for long periods of time, or a war rages with shocking violence and casualties—that you have lost all hope of a peaceful outcome. Ask your guardian angels to help you summon an image of a flock of doves. See them, in your mind's eye, flying to your loved ones or a war-torn land. With your angels' help, set the intention that when these doves reach their destination, they will work on the hearts of the people involved in this conflict and fill them not only with the desire for justice, but also for peace.

As a symbol of Spirit, the dove has the power to travel any-where, and bring along miracles on its wings. That's because Spirit can make the impossible possible. And we humans, often relating to and explaining life through symbol and metaphor, might need a concrete image to remind us of Spirit's power to transform and heal conflict. The dove is an embodiment of Spirit's supernatural ability to create peace.

Angel Affirmation: Whenever I need to embody grace, gentleness, and peace, I can ask my guardian angels to help me evoke the spirit of the dove, and send its image and message out into the world.

8

• ⎯⎯⎯⎯⎯⎯⎯⎯⎯

Angels & Love

A book on angels would not be complete without discussing love, for love is the fuel that angels run on. But it is not a saccharine sort of sentiment. Yes, angelic love is sweet and pure, but its hallmarks are sacrifice and devotion.

An angel's love is so strong that there are times an angel will allow you to fall on your face, if your angel knows this is for your highest good, even though it will hurt the angels very much to watch you suffer. And an angel will stand by you during your most trying moments, even when it means that your angel has to feel all the pain and frustration you are going through as if it were their own.

The angels tell me they feel your pain and frustration even more than you do. They don't say this to minimize your own suffering, but to try and help you better understand the angel realm. The angels show me they are so sensitive that it's as if their emotional outer layer is like the thin skin of a grape, almost transparent. Angels absorb so much of our emotions just being near us. Furthermore, angels agree to take on much of our pain when we are heartbroken, physically ill, fearful, or hurting in any way. The angels take this pain on despite the pain it causes them, because their love for us runs so deep. The angels are showing me that they are alchemists, and can take our pain on and turn it into something loving and pure and joyful, just as an alchemist can turn lead into gold. An angel's love is a love that is not tireless, yet pushes through exhaustion to remain loyally, steadfastly by your side. In short, an angel's love abides all things.

It is precious to us and greatly appreciated by the angels when we can return a bit of this love to them, just by sending our angels a kind thought, a simple thank you, or the message that we also deeply love our angels and Spirit. Angels are showing me an image of a small child giving its mother a hug by wrapping its tiny arms around the mother's legs. Boy, does that make a mom feel good! This is how angels feel when we send them a loving thank you or acknowledgment of their presence. Another fun way to do this is to ask your angels for a hug. You will feel an energy shift as their loving presence surrounds you. Savor that hug for a few moments, sending the angels love in return.

Angels Are Love

What does love look like in the angel realm, and is it different from how we experience love on earth?

Love *is* different in the angel realm. The angels' love is unconditional. There is nothing you can do to destroy or damage an angel's love for you. You can deny the existence of the angel realm, you can rail against fate and Spirit—the angels will still love you. This differs from earthly love, where someone can hurt you in a vicious and cruel way and it can most certainly damage your love for them!

The angels will also never abandon you. You may feel shame for things you've done, but your angels will be by your side, faithfully, more present than ever in your hours of need. Again, this differs from earthly love, where many times we may love someone dearly but for any number of reasons feel we can no longer be a part of their life.

The angels will always forgive you. That's because to Spirit, nothing is unforgivable. Think of the most unforgivable thing you have ever done (I know this can be painful). Do you have a clear picture of it? Here is your guardian angel's response: "I'm so sorry you have suffered so much over this memory. I know how much you regret hurting yourself and others. Understand that you are forgiven in the eyes of Spirit, totally and without reservation." (Take a moment to let that resonate with you and feel any emotions that come up.) I think forgiveness is one of the most powerful forces in the universe, but I'm a firm believer that humans don't have to forgive everything because sometimes it might be too hard or not feel genuine. Accepting and moving on can be just as powerful.

When you think of love in the angel realm this way—you are loved unconditionally, you will never be abandoned, you are always forgiven—love seems a dissolve lens, pastel vision of hearts and flowers. But there is more to love in the angel realm. Angels will still let you make mistakes. They will still let you suffer. They will allow your heart to break, and sometimes even guide you to situations to facilitate heartbreak. But that's because angels love you enough to want you to learn and grow into the most dynamic, wise version of yourself. Just as a devoted mother will allow her child to make mistakes, experience fear, and risk heartbreak and rejection, so will your angels allow you to feel pain. It hurts them to do it, because it hurts them to see you suffer (that's why they are closer than ever to you in times of crisis). Your guardian angels hate to see you crying into your pillow about a romantic love that ended, but the angels know a partner more suited to you is on their way. Sure, the angels could have tried to save this relationship, but it wasn't for your highest good.

Here on earth, I think love is a little more complex than in the angel realm. I do believe that the earth is moving toward a love that is similar to the love of the angel realm. Love that means everyone is treated fairly. Love that means everyone is entitled to mercy, even when their actions don't "deserve" it. Love that means treating others as you would want to be treated. Love is synonymous with angels because love is the highest vibrational energy in the universe, and angels are some of the highest vibrational beings in the universe. By high vibrational, I mean enlightened.

One thing you can count on is that when you need love, the angels are always there to provide it, no matter what. That's because, simply put, angels *are* love.

Angel Affirmation: My guardian angels love me unconditionally, will never abandon me, and will forgive me anything.

True Love

The angels urge us to celebrate romantic love for itself alone, and not to measure its significance or success by the outcome of a relationship. To love another where the love is unrequited, to have a love between two people end, or to be lovers separated by death are all sacred situations where we have glimpsed Spirit through the eyes of another human soul. For to fall in love with someone is to love them as the angels do—truly—and to see them through the eyes of an angel: beautiful and magnetic and utterly worthy of admiration.

If you fall in love with someone and the love is not returned, do not diminish your feelings by denying them. Just because the person you desire did not feel the same does not mean you are less worthy of love, nor does it negate the gift you bestowed by proving to your love that they are deserving of affection and adoration. Love offered to another is always true and never a waste, and your ability to care deeply for others should ever be a source of pride, never of shame or regret. The angels do want me to urge you to move on, though. Perhaps this person taught you how to love or how deeply you could love, or maybe you taught the object of your affection that they are worthy of love. But now you need to move on to someone who can love you back!

If two people fall out of love, the angels want you to trust that, on a soul level, you were brought together for a reason, to learn and grow and support each other, and that the need for your romantic union is over. Yet the love was still true. A relationship does not have to last forever to be a success. Not all loves are meant to stand the test of time. As you work through feelings of pain and anger, and seek out healing, try to hold on to that seed of love you once felt for your former partner, wishing them well, releasing them with grace, and allowing yourself to keep a small piece of them in your heart. True love never really fades to black. When two hearts have opened fully to each other once, they will always be linked on a soul level.

If you and your love were separated by death, the angels want you to take comfort in the knowledge that you will be reunited in heaven. As you grieve your loss, the angels want you to be thankful for the time you gained with one another on earth, and to treat those memories as your most precious possessions. You will see your love again on the other side, but you don't have to wait that long to hear from them. The angels want you to look out for messages from your love in animals, music, thoughts, and dreams, like letters from a friend who is far away. The angels want to assure you that your love now resides in a place made for lovers—a paradise of unconditional love. As your love watches you go about your life on earth, they want more than anything to see you happy, leading a dynamic life, and even being open to finding true love again. Your love is not lost, but working with your guardian angels to send you reminders of your love's presence and affection.

The important loves of your life were brought to you with the help of your guardian angels. Your guardian angels conspired with the guardian angels of your true love and together these two groups of angels acted as matchmakers. Many of these true-love relationships were already predestined, but your guardian angels made sure you and your love got together at the right time, in the right place, and for the right reasons— the reasons that would best serve both your souls.

If you want love in your life, ask your guardian angels to help. They might do this by contacting the guardian angels of a potential love, sending you guidance about steps you can take to better prepare yourself for a healthy relationship, offering intuitive information about what you may be doing unconsciously to block a love relationship, or suggesting activities and settings that might invite the right type of partner into your life.

Angel Affirmation: Romantic love never dies. To truly love means to have a love that lives forever, and is as eternal as the angels themselves.

Be a Romantic

Be a romantic—just like your angels. Romantics aren't naïve, looking at the world through rose-colored glasses that don't allow them to see life's inconvenient or troubling details. Nor are romantics fanciful, ascribing emotional depth and meaning to straightforward situations. In fact the exact opposite is true: Romantics see life in 3-D. They notice it all, they feel it all, they want to experience it all.

In this way romantics have much in common with angels. Divine angels and human romantics can both clearly see the hand of Spirit on a situation, intuitively know when two people have an important soul contract together, enjoy expressing affection for loved ones, don't shy away from painful or challenging situations, see the good in people, see great potential in every situation, and are very sensitive to the beauty and magic here on earth.

You'll know you're a romantic if you are deeply moved and touched by art, beauty, and music. If you are able to learn much about humanity and yourself through fictional books and films, and the characters seem alive and real to you. If friendships are very important, and many friends become family. If you glean philosophical insights from situations that others see as minor or forgettable. If you gain great joy from objects or presents that other people find token or ordinary. If you fall in love easily. If you are very passionate about your work or causes you believe in. If you are considered extraordinarily optimistic by your peers. If you believe people are good at heart and often give others the benefit of the doubt. If you think changing the world is possible. If you have a flare for the dramatic. If you "wear your heart on your sleeve." If you enjoy making grand displays of affection. If it's very easy for you to have intense conversations about the meaning of life, or it's easy for you to share details about your life that some would consider very personal, with people you just met. If you look for the larger meaning or lesson in situations. If you enjoy chatting for hours with friends about spirituality and the divine. If you have an adventurous streak and are more comfortable than most with taking risks. If it's easy for you to show affection and tell someone how much you care. If you love to comfort others and are generally very warm. If you laugh often and have a sharp sense of humor. If when you first discover something you like, you become a bit obsessed with it for a time, immersing yourself in it, only to then drop it and move on to something new. If you hate injustice and always fight for the underdog. If you are a committed activist.

In the past, you might have been made to feel silly or odd for being a romantic. People may have told you that you're too emotional or too passionate or just too *much*. That you aren't realistic. That you read too many things into a situation. That you make people out to be more interesting or colorful than they are. That you are too caring or a pushover.

Of course there is a shadow side to being a romantic, and working on boundaries—not taking on the emotions of others, not giving to others more than is good for you, taking even better care of yourself than you do of others, looking before you leap, taking calculated risks instead of foolish ones, being able to recognize when you are emotionally overwhelmed and need to ground yourself in activities that are dry and calming, getting plenty of rest, not trusting people blindly—is of the utmost importance for a romantic. But having a romantic disposition is nothing to be ashamed of or curbed. Rather, it is something to be envied and celebrated. For being a romantic really means engaging in the present moment with an inquisitive mind, an open heart, and all your senses alert and aware. Romantics are connoisseurs of life. In a nutshell, being a romantic means realizing you are a magical being on a magical journey on a magical planet. What an adventure! It's a way of viewing the human existence that your angels certainly share.

If you want more romance in your life, open your heart. Don't close off to people and opportunities because you have been hurt in the past, instead work on healthy boundaries, the angels are telling me. There is a major difference between shutting down your heart (the angels are showing me an image of someone pulling a plug out of a wall socket) and building a little fence around your heart with a gate that you can open and close. Romantics acknowledge and feel the pain in this life, but romantics look at pain as a necessary part of the journey, and can even sense a sliver of beauty in suffering. That's because romantics know that to feel deeply, even if those feelings sometimes hurt, means feeling alive. It means growing, learning, experiencing, and evolving. Likewise, romantics realize that to take an educated, intuitive-based risk always pays off, because adventure is thrilling no matter the outcome.

So if you're a romantic, you are in good company—the company of angels. And if you need to cultivate more romance, ask your guardian angels to help you slow down and see life for the lush, cinematic, 3-D adventure it was intended to be.

Angel Prayer: *Guardian angels, help me value and honor the romantic in me. Show me where I need to cultivate more romance, and aid me in healing, exploring, and expressing that sacred part of myself.*

9

Archangels

Think of archangels as the captains of the angel team. Are they better than other angels, or even more important? Of course not. Where would the captain of the team be without the other players? While archangels are extremely powerful and help to oversee other angels, every angel has its place and its need.

One benefit of calling in an archangel to help you is that they have a command over, so to speak, other angels, and can easily communicate with and rally these angels to your cause. And, of course, archangels are potent, as you will discover once you start working with them.

The angels tell me that archangels almost exist to represent an archetype, and have the ability to harness all the energy of that archetype. For Archangel Michael, this might be seen as the archetype of the protector. For Archangel Chamuel, this could be interpreted as the archetype of the peacemaker.

Working with Archangels

Many people are intimidated by the idea of asking archangels for assistance, because they feel these mighty spiritual giants surely have more important things to do than come to the aid of one individual. Your guardian angels, and the archangels themselves, want to set you straight on this. It is because the archangels are so commanding, capable, and strong that they can easily come to your aid. There is a reason these sacred entities are archangels—they are more than equal to the task of aiding every angel in heaven and every human on earth. It is also part of the mystery of faith that any archangel you call upon—or any ascended master such as Jesus, Mary, or Buddha—can be in all places at once. The archangels and ascended masters are not ruled by the limitations of this earthly plane, like we are. What you and I experience as hard and fast laws of time and space do not apply to these entities. An archangel can be kneeling beside you as you pray in your bedroom in North Carolina, and at the same moment the same archangel can be watching over a baby as she sleeps in a bedroom in Sydney, Australia.

And just because the archangels have a full dance card does not mean you will get a watered-down version of their care. When you call in an archangel to help you, or when an archangel sees that you need the exceptional level of aid and expertise that they can provide and comes to you of their own accord, the energy and assistance you receive are, again, potent. Archangels are strong medicine. Archangels will stay with you as long as you have a need, often, the angels are telling me, long after you initially call upon them for assistance. They will keep working on your behalf until the job is done.

I'll share some of my own experiences with archangels to illustrate these points.

There is a very old, very famous church near my home, and I sometimes go there to feel closer to Spirit, to absorb the spiritual patina of 170 years of worship. There's a small chapel in the back of this large church reserved for silent prayer. One day I sat in the chapel and looked around at the people near me who were deep in prayer or meditation, as well as those kneeling at the altar offering up the contents of their heart to Spirit in sacred reverence. It struck me just how many people, all across the world, rely on Spirit. How much people need from Spirit. How important, and sometimes even urgent, their prayers are. I suddenly felt so much compassion and love for all these people around me praying. *Spirit, I asked silently, please be here not just with me, but with everyone in this chapel who needs you so desperately. Please help these people and let them know they are never alone.* Suddenly I felt a presence, and I knew an energy force from the other side had entered the room. Usually I can get an intuitive hit on exactly who I'm sensing—a relative who has passed on, an angel, a spirit guide, an ascended master. But this time I was a bit paralyzed by the sheer size of the entity I was sensing. This was an enormous, powerful presence. Its energy was almost overwhelming. I realized it was an archangel. Archangel Gabriel had heard my prayer, and come to be with all these people in the chapel. Gabriel means "God is my strength," and I felt that strength. Wow, did I feel it! Gabriel is also the messenger archangel, and Gabriel's message to me that day was clear: Spirit is listening. Spirit is here for you, and here for all these people.

Another archangel, Michael, saw me through one of the scariest times in my life, when I was very ill and nervous about how to pay for the supplements and doctors I would need for my long healing journey. Having a financial crisis and a health crisis at the same time felt like more than I could handle. I knew I needed some extra help from heaven during this challenging period, so I enlisted Archangel Michael. Archangel Michael is kind and compassionate, but also brave. Archangel Michael specializes in helping people overcome fear. Often depicted with a sword, Archangel Michael is wonderful at providing courage, and courage was required to face what lay ahead for me. Anyone dealing with a life-threatening or chronic illness has to get in touch with their inner healer, but also their inner warrior. Michael gave me strength to go forward and fight for the help and resources I needed to heal. There were no two ways about it—I had to get tough, and Michael lent me some bravado. Also, knowing an archangel had my back gave me enormous peace of mind. I asked for Archangel Michael's assistance through prayer, and also gazed at a painting of this archangel carrying a sword, wearing a fierce expression, whenever I felt fear overwhelm me. I knew if this entity was in my corner, I was in good hands. I could face anything.

You can call on archangels for extra support, but often they are already supporting you behind the scenes without your knowledge, which was my experience with Archangel Uriel. A few years ago when I was working on my first book, *Heaven on*

Earth: A Guided Journal for Creating Your Own Divine Paradise, I spent lots of time and energy establishing myself as an author. Reaching out to people on social media, writing articles, working on book projects—I really came out swinging. As always, I constantly asked the angels for support, and I could feel their presence very consistently and intensely. I celebrated each victory with the angels, and I asked them for wisdom when things didn't go as I'd hoped. I honestly hadn't thought too much about the archangels, or any archangel in particular. But one day as I was thinking about writing this section of the book on archangels, I silently asked the angel realm which archangels shared a special connection to me. Suddenly the name Uriel was spoken into my ear, clear and certain. *Of course*, I thought. Uriel helps with ideas and creativity, especially as they relate to the Divine. Uriel can work to deliver big spiritual insights, the kind of insights I was trying to put into my books and deliver to others. Uriel had been helping me all along, giving me ideas even though I didn't consciously realize it or ask for this help. Let me tell you,though, Uriel got a big thank you the day I realized how indebted I was to this archangel, and Uriel deserves another thank you right now for closely guiding me through writing this book.

The following are archangels you might call upon to help you, or who might choose to work with you all on their own. Like doctors, they each have a specialty.

Archangel Ariel

Archangel Ariel, meaning "lion of God," is closely connected with nature, nature spirits like fairies, and wild animals. Call on Archangel Ariel for help with environmental activism projects; raising people's awareness of the need for conservation, recycling, organic farming, and other green practices; or to get ideas about how you as an individual can better protect, preserve, and honor nature.

Ariel's message is: *Pray for the healing of the earth, but also do more than pray. Examine your life and find ways to honor this sacred planet by taking practical steps to conserve its resources. It is time for a shift, for humans to take little from and give much to the earth and all its plant and animal inhabitants. Don't lose hope over the fate of Gaia, but do not sit idle. For if you sit idle, the future of this paradise is in serious jeopardy.*

Archangel Azrael

Archangel Azrael, meaning "one whom God helps," helps humans during the transition from earth to heaven. Archangel Azrael can calm and comfort the dying, smooth the transition from this life to the next, or help grieving loved ones cope with their loss. Azrael can also help you through the grieving and transition process of any type of loss: job, romantic, financial, etc.

Azrael's message is: *Do not fear death, or any other type of loss, for it is but the start of another life. And do not fear for loved ones who have passed, for they are in the timeless embrace of Spirit. All reunions are possible and will happen at the appointed hour. Until then, await a reunion with your departed loved one patiently, but do not wait to love again.*

Archangel Chamuel

Archangel Chamuel, meaning "one who sees God," is just like this sweet-sounding name: peaceful. If you are worried about a far-off war, or just a minor disagreement in your family, ask that Chamuel's intensely warm, soft, loving energy be with the situation and inspire your own actions. Chamuel can help you forgive others or forgive yourself, and has the ability to bring more love to any relationship.

Chamuel's message: *Find the softness and tenderness in life. Find the gentleness and healing. And when you find these things, give them to others. Feel all the love inside you, and all the love flowing throughout the world. Feel the enormous, intoxicating love I have for you, Spirit's child, and know that this love comes straight from Spirit.*

Archangel Gabriel

Archangel Gabriel, meaning "God is my strength," is a messenger. Ask Archangel Gabriel to bring you messages directly from Spirit. Artists, healers, teachers, writers, politicians, activists, and anyone else who is communicating a message through their work can ask Gabriel to help them craft and deliver their messages to the world. Gabriel is also associated with children, helping from conception and even before, the angels tell me, as Gabriel can help a spirit in heaven pick out its future parents. Gabriel can also aid children on earth, especially the "downtrodden," the angels tell me, or any child who is needy like a sick child.

Archangel Gabriel's message: *Let the ideas and words of Spirit flow through you to bless humanity. I will bring those messages to you from Spirit, and I will work quickly and urgently to help you deliver those messages to the masses, to the fallen, to the forgotten, to the few, to the passionate, and to the many. I will help you craft, communicate, and spread your own message, for you have been chosen to do so. Call on me to help any child, especially those who are suffering.*

Archangel Haniel

Archangel Haniel, meaning "the grace of God," helps humans strengthen our mystical bond to Spirit and recall ancient, eternal wisdom. Haniel also teaches us to carry ourselves with a regal air of grace and poise, helpful if you are networking, organizing a large event, or often in the public eye. Haniel reminds us of the divine feminine and the worship of the goddess.

Haniel's message: *There is a greater knowledge and meaning to all things that you have instant access to. It is your birthright as a spiritual being. I can help you recall this eternal wisdom and power and magic. Carry yourself as the spiritual royalty you are: with grace and majesty and assurance and deft. Whenever you forget you are magnificent, call on me to help you remember you are royalty.*

Archangel Jeremiel

Archangel Jeremiel, meaning "God's mercy," offers humans mercy in the form of psychic messages. Archangel Jeremiel can send you knowledge through dreams and visions, and help you get in touch with your own psychic and intuitive abilities. Jeremiel can also help you discover your soul's purpose in this life and guide you to making better decisions about how to fulfill and live that purpose.

Jeremiel's message: *I offer you the aid of my psychic gifts, and help you to hone your own. Value these psychic gifts, mine and yours, for this sixth sense is how you make direct contact with the Divine. Living with an active and healthy sixth sense is the marriage of the world of Spirit and earth. Each human has an important and meaningful purpose on this planet. You were born with this purpose. It is written in the stars and across your heart. I can help you make the most of your mission on earth and reach your highest potential.*

Archangel Jophiel

Archangel Jophiel, meaning "beauty of God," wants us to recognize the power and importance of beauty, as beauty is high-vibrational and brings us closer to Spirit. Jophiel encourages us to incorporate more beauty into our homes, our wardrobes, our workplaces, our attitudes. Jophiel inspires and nurtures creators of beauty, especially those in the arts.

Jophiel's message: *When you are overwhelmed by beauty, you are seeing Spirit. Let beauty drench your senses and cleanse your soul. Worship it, embrace it, create it. Don't deny yourself beauty, and never deny it to others, for beauty must be accessible to all. Beauty feeds the soul and nourishes the spirit. Beauty is necessary, beauty is a reflection of Spirit, beauty is a window into the Divine. Those who dedicate their lives to creating beauty have taken holy orders, and do Spirit's work in the world.*

Archangel Metatron

Archangel Metatron, sometimes called the "angel of life" because this archangel is charged with recording history in the Book of Life or Akashic Records, was once human. Metatron understands the human condition in a unique way and therefore acts as a mediator or interpreter between heaven and earth, helping humans see their lives from a more spiritual perspective as well as providing us with knowledge about the afterlife.

Metatron's message: *I have seen the other side and know there is nothing to fear. I bring the peace and love of the afterlife to you, to illuminate your earthly existence and comfort you as you perform your sacred dance with Spirit on this earth. I have walked your path as a human, and know your pain and suffering, know your doubts and anxieties. Think of me as a wise elder, who assures you that this life has meaning and purpose, and that the life awaiting you beyond this one shall be glorious and filled with love.*

Archangel Michael

Archangel Michael, meaning "who is like God," is a warrior angel. If you are feeling paralyzed by fear and doubt, Michael can lend you courage. If you are anxious and confused about the next steps you should take in a situation, Michael can use his heavenly sword to cut through deception and vagueness to reveal the truth and choices that will lead to your highest good. Michael will help motivate you to take bold actions and move swiftly in the right direction. Michael is an excellent archangel to call upon when you are facing big decisions or a major crisis. Michael will make you feel brave, confident, empowered, decisive, safe, and protected.

Michael's message: *There is nothing to fear when I am by your side, and I am walking next to you now with my sword of light at the ready. There is nothing on earth you need fear when you are under my care, for I embody the strength and grace and wisdom of heaven. I am only one, yet my power and might is so great that I am like an army. When you face your greatest challenges, I will be there to guide and protect you. I am loyal, trustworthy, and honorable, like a knight of old. I fight for what is right and fair. I will awaken the warrior in you, the part of your soul that does not run from challenges but relishes the battle. Together you and I are a force to be reckoned with.*

Archangel Raguel

Archangel Raguel, meaning "friend of God," is a champion for equality, fairness, justice, and mercy. More than judging or condemning, Raguel fights for the rights of the oppressed and the underdogs. Raguel stands for the morality of kindness, compassion, and charity. Raguel knows that all humans are created equal, and wants to see a more equal distribution of the world's wealth and resources. Raguel is concerned with mercy, but if there is evil in the hearts of men, Raguel will work to swiftly end any unnecessary pain and suffering inflicted by one human upon another living creature. Whether you are an activist fighting for social reform on a large scale or simply aiding a single individual, Raguel is with you. Raguel is a natural leader, and, the angels tell me, can help you with your leadership skills and charisma.

Raguel's message: *Search your heart, and think from that space rather than from your head. How can you help those who are suffering or unfairly treated? Answer that question and you unlock the kingdom of heaven on earth. Teach those with strength and power that it is their sacred duty to care for the meek and the gentle and the sick. See Spirit in every other living creature. See Spirit in yourself, and act from that holy place of mercy, equality, and love. If you see that someone has not been given the advantages you were born with, go out of your way to help them. This dimension is moving more and more toward an enlightened equality, and you have been born now to play your part in fighting for justice for all.*

Archangel Raphael

Archangel Raphael, meaning "God heals," is an expert at healing emotional, physical, and spiritual illnesses. Raphael is the patron of all professional healers, and helps guide the hearts, hands, and minds of naturopaths, surgeons, pharmacists, nutritionists, energy workers, and therapists in their practices. Raphael is also present whenever we offer healing words, love, and care to family or friends. And if we're the ones who are sick, Raphael will send us dreams and intuitive insights about which doctors and supplements and healing modalities can best help us.

Raphael's message: *Do not despair if you are sick, for the healing wonders of the universe are infinite. Unless you are meant to die, and the predestined end of your earthly journey is upon you, physical, emotional, and spiritual healing are available to you. If you are having trouble connecting with the right doctor or healing method, call on me to help guide you and bring the right people and resources and knowledge into your life. If you are in the healing professions, call on me before each session, and let me work through you to bring an exceptional level of care to your patients and clients. Remember, to be a patient is not a passive role but an interactive one, a partnership between you, your healthcare providers, and Spirit.*

Archangel Raziel

Archangel Raziel, meaning "secret of God," can help you gain a greater understanding and mastery of mysticism, the power of magic, and the ability to manifest. Raziel is a spiritual scholar who aids those with a natural inclination to study heady, esoteric spiritual texts, and also guides humans toward spiritual books and tools as each individual becomes ready to reach higher levels of enlightenment. Raziel wants to assure us that magic and manifesting are tools for good, and that anyone trying to use these skills selfishly or to harm another will be halted and hindered by the wisdom and power of Spirit. Raziel will no longer act as a guide to these misguided individuals, but rather a roadblock. Raziel can also help you improve your psychic abilities, such as clairvoyance and clairaudience.

Raziel's message: *Each of us has a bit of the wizard inside, the ability to pray over a situation and affect its outcome. This power should always be intended for the highest good of yourself and others, never for harm. Those attempting to use God's gifts of manifestation for harm will only succeed in harming themselves. Remember that the world is a magical place, full of mystery and wonder. Embrace that fact, for it is what makes the world compelling. All things under the sun are under the constant supervision and light of Spirit. Play with manifesting, for this is how you create. And trust that whatever form your intention takes, it is always for your highest good, and the highest good of those around you.*

Archangel Sandalphon

Archangel Sandalphon, meaning "angel of prayer," was once a human, like the Archangel Metatron. Also like Metatron, Sandalphon acts as a bridge between heaven and earth. Sandalphon specializes in delivering human's prayers to heaven, as well as delivering the answers to those prayers. If you have a very important prayer, ask that Sandalphon send it quickly and clearly up to heaven. If you are having trouble understanding or recognizing the answer to your prayer, ask Sandalphon to help you interpret Spirit's response. Sandalphon has a special relationship with music, so music might be one way this archangel reveals Spirit's guidance to you.

Sandalphon's message: *Every prayer is heard and, in its own unique way, answered. Believe in the enormous power of prayer. Stay open-minded when looking for Spirit's answers to your prayers, and try not to be attached to a specific outcome. If you are confused about the guidance Spirit gives you after praying, or have difficulty seeing the wisdom in Spirit's answer to your prayer, call on me to help interpret the language of heaven.*

Archangel Uriel

Archangel Uriel, meaning "God is my light," shines light on the world in the form of prophecy. Uriel brings big spiritual insights to the world, heralds the coming of innovative spiritual leaders, and can even warn us of major future events, including catastrophes. When you have questions about philosophy and the meaning of life, call on Uriel for insight. Uriel can shed light on any question or problem, no matter how large or complex.

Uriel's message: *Seek me out for help with life's big spiritual and philosophical dilemmas. I will aid those who are spiritual leaders, teachers, thinkers, and writers so they may impart to others great spiritual knowledge and truth. My wisdom is dramatic and profound, for it comes straight from Spirit and is encoded with the next level of enlightenment for the planet.*

Archangel Zadkiel

Archangel Zadkiel, meaning "righteousness of God," is all about mercy and forgiveness. In the eyes of Spirit, nothing is unforgivable. Zadkiel can help you forgive yourself, forgive others, and move on from and heal emotional wounds when you find forgiveness too difficult. Zadkiel reminds us that every living creature, no matter what they have done, is worthy of mercy, and that inflicting pain upon someone in an act of vengeance does nothing but add even more pain to the weight of the world.

Zadkiel's message: *I will be with those in the justice system and law enforcement to make sure they not only keep society safe and protected, but also to encourage mercy in all forms of sentencing and punishment. Work on forgiveness, but do not punish yourself when you find forgiveness too difficult. Let Spirit forgive those you cannot forgive, and work instead in healing yourself and moving on.*

10

———•———

Leaning on Angels
When Life Is Hard

Earthly life is not for the faint of heart! No matter who you are or what your circumstances, no human is spared pain and challenges as aspects of their journey. It's simply part of the gig.

But one of the angels', and especially your guardian angels', main tasks is to help comfort and guide you through these challenging, painful seasons. When you are feeling scared, sad, defeated, or confused, get in the habit of immediately contacting your guardian angels. They can offer you comfort, wisdom, practical guidance, and in some cases even dramatic intervention.

Make it your default response to reach out to angels when life gets hard. The hard times are *always* easier to handle with help from the angels.

Let Angels Help You Process
and Move Through Difficult Emotions

There is great spiritual and emotional value is sitting with difficult emotions. However, it can be uncomfortable and painful to allow yourself to feel and examine emotions like sadness and anger. The angels want you to know that you won't have to sit with these emotions alone—your guardian angels will be right by your side. Also by your side will be a group of healing helper angels who specialize in emotional health. These angels will give you the strength and courage to process your emotions. They will also soothe you along the journey and help you access the information your emotions are trying to convey. (You should never feel shy about seeing a professional counselor for emotional help, too. Many times, angels alone are not enough.)

We tend to avoid our difficult emotions because leaning into them simply doesn't feel so hot. Sadness breaks our heart, and anger can make us feel frustrated and out of control. But the angels want us to know that feeling *all* our emotions, even the difficult ones, is an essential part of our human journey. To bury our difficult emotions or distance ourselves from them is like seeing a classic movie but fast-forwarding through all the sad, tense parts. Those sections of the film inform the story and give it depth and meaning. If you don't watch the whole thing, you won't really experience the movie at all. If you don't process your difficult emotions, you aren't really present for this magnificent movie your soul is starring in! And trust me, it's a classic.

Not processing difficult emotions can also cause health problems. These emotions become toxic to you emotionally *and* physically. They might cause or exacerbate illness in your body, and they might stunt your emotional growth and your relationships with others. If you don't admit to your pain, you cannot seek out real healing from healthcare professionals, loved ones, or even Spirit.

Processing your difficult emotions is the only way to learn the valuable information these emotions are trying to convey. Anger might teach you a lesson about your boundaries—we often discover where our boundaries are when they are crossed. Anger can also teach you what is important to you, where you stand on an ethical situation, and what you want to change about the world. Sadness can teach you how much something or someone means to you. Sadness can let you know when you are off track in your life purpose or when something vital is missing from your life. (If you're having trouble figuring out the message or messages behind an emotion, ask your angels for help. They will usually give you a sense of the message or whisper the answer into your mind.)

Processing and sitting with difficult emotions can look like: crying, laughing, beating a pillow, doing some type of physical exercise, talking to a loved one about your feelings, talking to a counselor or therapist or life coach, confronting a person who hurt you and expressing your feelings to them (once you have calmed down, and only if the person is safe to confront), holding a ceremony, journaling about your feelings, talking to your angels, taking action steps to change the situation that is upsetting you, or taking some other appropriate form of action. When you make a commitment to feel your difficult emotions and process them, the angels will send you helpful guidance, such as books or movies or people who can offer wisdom. And remember, you can do this at your own pace, the angels want me to tell you. You don't have to let the feelings completely overwhelm you. You can examine them in short sessions over time until you've worked through the meat of the emotion/situation.

If you don't process and sit with these difficult emotions, it is very hard to move past them. This is one reason people have trouble forgiving. Allowing yourself to feel hurt or angry, confronting the person who upset you, and expressing your emotions in a calm and safe way (if talking to them isn't safe or isn't an option, you can always write them a letter and then tear it up), and talking the whole situation through with a loved one or counselor does *miraculous* things for your ability to forgive.

If feelings of depression or rage seem to linger even after you have tried to process through them, see a healthcare professional. You may be suffering from a chemical imbalance, hormone imbalance, vitamin deficiency, or other medical condition. Or perhaps what is behind the sadness or anger is a larger issue, possibly even dating back to childhood, that will require the help of a healthcare professional to process and heal. Or this might be just a very large wound with a lot of emotional scar tissue that, again, requires a professional's help. On a personal note, I must admit that I love talk therapy, and have utilized professional counselors and coaches to help me with emotional maintenance. You don't have to be in a crisis to seek these folks out or benefit from their assistance. And you don't have to work with a healthcare professional *or* the angels. You can work with both, and the angels are telling me they "encourage" you to work with both.

Sometimes sadness and anger can linger longer than is useful, even once you have successfully processed through them. If this is the case, the angels are telling me it's like "residual, old energy" hanging around that needs to be cleared. You can always ask the angels to help lift this emotion from you. Go to a quiet place where you will be alone. Contact an angel (you could ask for one of your guardian angels, an archangel, or one of the healing helper angels that deals with emotions). Then think, "Dear angel, please take away this painful, heavy feeling. Let me experience lightness and joy again." It is astonishing how quickly an angel can change your mood, and how dramatically your feelings of malaise can turn to delight. (I have experienced this immediately after praying many times.) But remember, if this mood is trying to tell you something, or you have not processed through your feelings yet, an angel will not change it for you.

The angel realm wants you to know that one of the best motivations for processing your difficult emotions is that this will enhance your more pleasurable ones too. When we hold difficult emotions at bay, we begin to numb ourselves to emotions of joy and wonder as well. When you close off your heart to difficult emotions, you will not experience joy and wonder with the same depth and intensity. And the angels want you to feel joy and wonder fully and completely. You deserve it!

Angel Prayer: Healing angels, I want help processing my difficult emotions. Please send me guidance on how I can work on this, and how I can do this in a safe way and in my own time.

Angel Exercise:
Get in Touch with the Emotions of a Heavy Heart

You may have been putting off processing difficult or negative emotions because you are too busy, or because you feel you have to soldier through the challenges you are facing. Perhaps you fear the emotions are so disturbing that you will drown in them, or you think you need to be strong for a loved one. Maybe (this is usually on a subconscious level) you don't feel you deserve comfort and solace. You might believe these painful emotions will naturally disappear when the situation that instigated them is resolved (in actuality when the painful situation is resolved these emotions often become more intense and nearer the surface, as you now have the time and space to deal with them more fully). Possibly no one has ever taught you the value of processing negative emotions or shown you how to go about doing it.

The angels want you to know it is not only safe to experience these negative emotions, but it is necessary. If you don't, your heart will become heavy, and it won't work properly—in an emotional sense. Once you begin to process these emotions you will feel more strength and peace. As you start processing more recent emotions, emotions long buried and never processed, from as far back as childhood, will likely begin to surface.

Your guardian angels want you to do this exercise as often as you need, or routinely a few times a year as "heart maintenance." Your guardian angels are never too busy for you, their number-one project, and delight in standing by you as you perform exercises like this one. Angels love to do work on your heart since your heart is the engine that fuels your compassion, tenderness, and love, and therefore is very closely linked to the angel realm.

It's best to do this exercise with a journal. Ask yourself the following questions, but first, with all the exercises in this section of the book, say a prayer either aloud or silently that the answers you receive will be from the angel realm and from your higher self, the part of you that is closely connected to Spirit and an eternal wisdom. Try to make your mind very still and calm as you ask yourself these questions, and wait to hear answers. If you have trouble quieting your mind, ask your guardian angels for help. We're going fishing now, and we don't want to scare off the best catches with a bunch of chatter! Some of the answers you receive will be things you already know but have been avoiding, and others will be brilliant ideas that come as a total shock to your conscious mind, originating from a place further inside yourself—or straight from your guardian angels.

Place your hand over your heart. Feel the warmth of it through your chest, feel the rhythmic, primal beat of it in your bones. Take a few moments to close your eyes and get in touch with your physical and emotional heart. Once you are grounded in heart energy you might feel more vulnerable, more peaceful, more loving, or more emotional. You should definitely feel a change.

Then ask yourself, "What is weighing heaviest on my heart right now?" Write any answers that come in your journal. If you feel the need to cry or comfort yourself with a hug at any point, stop and do so. Your guardian angels are close by right now, helping you uncover answers, giving you courage, and sending you love. Healing helper angels who specialize in emotional health are probably also present now.

Keep your hand over your heart for all the following questions, and next ask: "What am I afraid of most right now?" Write down the answers in your journal.

Next ask, "What is causing me the most pain and sadness right now?" Write down the answers in your journal.

Next ask, "Why am I resisting the intense emotions I am feeling?" Write down any answers.

Next ask, "What do I use to avoid, bury, or deny my feelings?" Write down any answers.

Next ask, "How am I downplaying the emotions I am feeling either to myself or to those around me?" Write down any answers.

Next ask, "Who am I trying to protect by burying or denying my negative feelings?" Write down any answers.

Next ask, "Is there someone who taught me to bury emotions as a coping mechanism when I was a child or once I became an adult?" Write down any answers.

Next ask, "How can I safely begin to process these emotions?" Write down any answers.

Next ask, "How can I process these emotions at a pace that feels manageable and safe to me?" Write down any answers.

Next ask, "What lessons do these painful emotions want to teach me about myself, self-care, boundaries, activism, change, life, my relationships, my work, or love?" Write down any answers.

Next ask, "What else does my heart want to express about the pain I am feeling?" Write down any answers.

Finally ask, "What messages does my heart have for me that I have not been willing to hear until now?" Write down any answers.

ANGEL EXERCISE:
GAINING SUPPORT WHEN THE HEART IS HEAVY

The second heavy-heart exercise helps you identify ways you can support yourself, and seek support from others, as you process through these painful emotions. The exercise also offers ideas for how you might add a bit of lightness to that heavy heart you've been walking around with. Again, this exercise can be done without a journal but it's helpful to have one.

1. How can I give myself more space and time to deal with my heavy heart?

2. Which loved ones and healthcare professionals could help me cope right now with my heavy heart?

3. What boundaries do I need to set to protect my heart right now?

4. What is my biggest fear about processing the emotions that are weighing my heart down?

5. Who in my life is the most supportive when I'm feeling down?

6. Who in my life do I need to protect myself from when I'm feeling down?

7. Do I consciously or subconsciously think there is an advantage to bottling up my emotions? If so, what?

8. What are some of the obvious negative consequences of bottling up my emotions, both mental and physical?

9. What or whom in my life feels so emotionally overwhelming right now that I need to take a break from them/it?

10. Is there someone in my life who is in crisis and whom I feel I am emotionally "carrying" right now?

11. Is there someone in my life who seems to thrive off drama, or who likes to dump their emotions on me?

12. Is there a specific person I need to create better boundaries with?

13. Have I always been emotionally sensitive? Do I feel things more deeply than others appear to, and/or is it easy for me to absorb the feelings of those around me?

14. Have I been viewing my emotional sensitivity as a weakness and a burden, or as a gift and a strength that comes with some downsides and challenges?

15. What are some small things that are bringing me joy and satisfaction in my life right now?

16. What is at least one big thing that is going well in my life right now?

17. What feels easy or effortless in my life right now?

18. What do I feel hopeful about right now?

19. What is usually a guaranteed way to make me laugh?

20. What activities make me feel free?

21. Have I been touching base with my angels, and asking them for more love and guidance?

22. Have I been on the lookout for signs and messages from my angels? Are there any messages from my angels that might have been delivered through friends, family, coworkers, or even strangers?

Angel Exercise:
Angels Can Help Carry Your Heavy Heart

This next exercise is ideal for when you or a loved one is in crisis, and the intense emotions swirling around your little world are not likely to settle down anytime soon. During these periods a heart heavy with negative or difficult emotions needs help simply moving forward through life, one beat at a time.

In a room where you can be alone, close the door and block out noise and get in a comfortable position, either seated on

the floor or lying down on a bed or couch. Address the angels
out loud in a soft, calm voice: "Angels, I have had so many painful, intense emotions lately that I need your help carrying this
heavy heart. I know you are always with me, but I am asking for
extra assistance right now. I realize that I am never a burden to
you, and that you delight in my call for aid. Give it to me now,
and let me feel the benefits of your help immediately."

The following is a guided meditation. Read a few sentences, and then close your eyes and spend a minute picturing
what you have read. When you have spent enough time on that
image, open your eyes and move on to the next one:

1. Picture yourself surrounded by angels. You see their
   flowing robes, their magnificent wings. Most of all you
   notice their expressions as they gaze upon you. They
   gently stare at you with affection, and wise eyes that say
   they know how much you have suffered.

2. The angels fly or float slowly closer. Soon they form a
   circle around you, hovering in place. One by one they
   spin around, each shaking a few feathers from their
   wings. The angels smile as they do this, for it does not
   cause them pain. They have plenty of feathers to spare
   and are happy to gift you these celestial presents.

3. A large pile of feathers has accumulated, and the angels
   gather them up and place them under your feet, so that
   you are floating on top of these downy, white feathers.
   Suddenly you feel lighter, like the feathers are carrying you.

4. One of the angels extends her arm and magically pushes you off on your feather bed, and you set sail through
   the air. You are now back in your daily routine: going
   to work, cleaning your house, taking care of friends and
   family, although instead of plodding along using all of
   your energy to move through your days, the angels are
   carrying you as you float on your bed of magic feathers.

Meditate for five minutes, or longer if you choose, on these
images and the feelings they bring up. You might picture the
details of your daily routine at home or at work, floating on your
angel feathers. Or picture a stressful situation you've been dealing
with, now handling it from the soft comfort and support of your
bed of angel feathers.

Angel Exercise:
Allow Guardian Angels to
Fill Your Heart with Hope & Love

Now that we have done some work on processing the heavy,
painful emotions you have been carrying, there is room in your
heart to add even more lightness. Since your heart became
heavy with these painful emotions, you might have lost touch
with many of the joys and blessings of your daily life, and most
probably have lost touch with a sense of hope for the future. As
always, your guardian angels can help!

In a room where you can be alone, close the door, and block
out noise, get in a comfortable position, either seated on the floor
or lying down on a bed or couch.

Address the angels out loud in a soft, calm voice:

"Guardian angels, please reveal the current blessings in my life, from which I may draw pleasure and strength."

Quietly listen for any answers. These might come to you as thoughts, mental images, feelings, or words spoken into your ear directly from your angels. Once you feel the angels have given you their answers, you might want to record these answers in your journal.

Now ask, "Guardian angels, which people or situations in my life should I feel more hopeful about?"

Quietly listen for answers, and record them in your journal.

Now ask, "Guardian angels, who can I hang out with or talk to on the phone to make me laugh?"

Quietly listen for answers, and record them in your journal.

Now ask, "Guardian angels, which chores or duties can I take off my plate so that I have more time to play and do activities that make me smile?"

Quietly listen for answers, and record them in your journal.

Now ask, "Guardian angels, who in my life is stronger than I think?"

Quietly listen for answers, and record them in your journal.

Now ask, "Guardian angels, what surprising blessings does the near future hold for me?"

Quietly listen for answers, and record them in your journal.

Now ask, "Guardian angels, what surprising blessings can I look forward to in the distant future?"

Quietly listen for answers, and record them in your journal.

Now ask, "Guardian angels, how can I find more joy in my daily life?"

Quietly listen for answers, and record them in your journal.

Now ask, "Guardian angels, what in my life right now should I be celebrating?"

Quietly listen for answers, and record them in your journal.

Now ask, "Guardian angels, who in my life really believes in me?"

Quietly listen for answers, and record them in your journal.

Epic Challenges

When you experience challenges, it does not mean that God is punishing you, or that your angels have abandoned you. Quite the opposite: Many struggles you face in life are brought to you straight from Spirit, at the exact moment when God and the angels know you are ready to grow and evolve by facing an epic challenge. The fact that you are being challenged only shows the faith that your guardian angels have in your ability to now walk through the fire with grace and courage. You may not feel ready for this epic challenge, and you might even go kicking and screaming at first, before eventually settling into a grudging acceptance of your fate. But your angels know you are ready to summon forth those undiscovered/uncharted parts of yourself that can rise to this occasion and will grow from the experience.

No life is ordinary, or unimportant, thus your existence deserves the same drama, emotion, and adventure as a knight on a quest in an ancient fairy tale. A good story has conflict, and characters that change and evolve—your story is no different (and is the most important story you will ever know or tell). The same precious metal that made up Martin Luther King Jr., Susan B. Anthony, and even Jesus Christ is what your soul was forged in. Yet some of your greatest assets—patience, talent, bravery, activism, leadership, resolve, loyalty, faith, compassion, wisdom—may lie dormant until activated by an epic challenge sent to you from Spirit.

An illness you face could teach you how to heal others. A loss you suffer could make you more compassionate to the suffering of every living creature. An injustice you or a family member endures could inspire you to become a powerful activist. Whether the challenge you face ends up helping you, thousands of strangers, or simply one other person does not matter. The angels want you to always remember that every act of love and kindness, however small, holds within it the power to change the world.

When you face a challenge, your angels will be there to bring you the opportunities, people, and resources you require. They will also help you activate and bring forth the inner qualities you need, just as Arthur found he had the power to pull a magical sword from a stone, and just as Jesus had the ability to turn water into wine.

Angel Affirmation: When I face an epic challenge, my angels will help me discover the epic courage, grace, ability, and opportunity to rise to the occasion.

The Benefits of Surrender

Your guardian angels want to gently remind you that sometimes attaching to outcome can be the most stressful part of a stressful situation. It's natural and healthy to have goals, pray for what you want, and put your shoulder to the wheel as you work toward your desires. But when plans don't turn out as you anticipated, and the outcome of cherished dreams seem uncertain, it's a sign you need to surrender the situation to Spirit.

There are huge, practical benefits of surrender. First, it's a relief. Stop strategizing toward a specific outcome. Take the appropriate action steps, mulling over the situation only as much as is productive, and then give your mind a break. Likewise, you need an emotional rest from the yearning you have been feeling for a specific "happy ending."

Surrendering also allows your angels to better work their magic. Once the mighty human will has been made to heel, you free up mental space for your angels to whisper words of comfort and wisdom into your brain, and for you to recognize and act upon this guidance. These angelic ideas might be key for a kind of happy ending of some sort, even if it's not the one you previously envisioned. And when you aren't so emotionally distraught it's easier for the angels to do healing energy work on you. Just as it's easier for a doctor to work on a patient who isn't struggling on the table, so is it easier for angels to work with you when you surrender. Also, once your powerful free will isn't trying to force a specific outcome, the universe is freed up to bring you a different, often better and more appropriate outcome!

Just because you surrender the outcome of a situation to Spirit, doesn't mean you stop praying. Instead of praying for exact ways the situation might resolve itself, pray for grace, wisdom, mercy, and miracles. And don't get too hung up on what those will look like when they appear, or how or when they will come.

Surrendering is an exercise of trust between you and Spirit. You are holding up your end of the bargain by taking action steps to resolve the situation as best you know how and by following the guidance of your guardian angels, but without forcing an outcome or specific set of circumstances and staying open-minded. Spirit and your angels always have your highest good in mind, and will work with you to make your highest good, or highest potential, a reality. Trust your guardian angels right now, as emissaries of Spirit, to shine a light in the darkness, and show you the most advantageous path forward—it may not be the same path you've been trodding.

> *Angel Prayer: Guardian angels, send me mercy, wisdom, grace, and miracles as I surrender the outcome of this situation to Spirit and my highest good.*

Angel Exercise:
Forgiveness with the Angel Realm

Angels forgive immediately, completely, and unconditionally. This is not how humans experience forgiveness, and that's okay. Angels can see all of us: our past wounds, our challenges, our intentions, our full spectrum of emotions regarding a situation, our souls. And angels are telling me that one of the biggest differences between them and us is: Angels "don't take things personally." That makes it much easier for angels to forgive us. Angels see humans as children, and like a devoted parent, an angel knows that humans sometimes do things to hurt others simply because we don't know better. And angels live in heaven, a dimension of love, where forgiveness is much more intrinsic—more "natural," the angels tell me.

Often humans need a little help forgiving, and we can borrow some angel dust to do so. Other times we may need to accept that forgiveness is not possible, at least not right now. When someone has wounded us or a loved one very deeply, it is best perhaps to work on accepting the wound, and expressing the feelings of sadness, disappointment, and anger that come with it. Once we express and explore our feelings, we can begin to move on from this wound and, if appropriate, the person who hurt us. I believe true forgiveness is not always possible or necessary. Healing, however, is always possible and necessary.

When forgiveness is possible, it's important not to use it as an excuse to ignore painful feelings, or the wound that caused them. The first step in honestly forgiving someone is expressing your emotions. You must admit and express these emotions to yourself—and preferably to a third party as well, like a therapist or loved one. I think it's also important to let someone know they hurt you before you can really forgive them. This isn't always possible (perhaps communicating with them directly would put you or someone else in danger). If the person who hurt you has passed on, you can express your painful emotions to them in a letter or a prayer. They will be listening from heaven, I can assure you of that.

The following exercise will engage the angel realm to help you forgive someone who hurt you. (Before performing this exercise, spend some time exploring and expressing your emotions about the person who hurt you and what they did.) For this exercise, choose a person who has recently upset you, or someone you have been trying to forgive, maybe even for years, but just can't. Focus on one person at a time. You can perform this exercise as often as you want, for as many people as you need help forgiving. You might want to do this exercise with a journal—especially if this is a big wound or a person who is integral to your life—where you can write down and record any insights.

First go into a room where you can be alone and shut a door. Quiet your mind and assume a comfortable position sitting up.

Say the following out loud: Guardian angels and any other angels who are experts at emotional healing and forgiveness, please be with me now as I work to forgive someone who hurt me.

Now state the name of the person you want to forgive (first name is enough), and then recount how this person hurt you.

Now explain to the angels how this incident made you feel. Take your time and explore some of your emotions. If you need to vent or to cry, that's not only healthy but expressing your emotions around this situation will actually make it easier for you to forgive. Give yourself as much time as you need with this step.

Tell the angels why you are having trouble forgiving this person. (Some reasons might be: You're still upset by what this person did, or this person never apologized, or you're afraid if you forgive them this person will only hurt you again, or you're afraid forgiving them will be like saying what they did was okay.)

Ask the angel realm the following: Dear angels, Why did [name] hurt me? Quiet your mind and be alert to any answers from the angel realm regarding this question. You might hear the answers in your mind, get a gut feeling, have an insightful thought enter your head, see an image that offers answers, or just receive a sudden knowing.

Ask the angel realm the following: *Dear Angels, Does [name] realize how badly I was hurt by their actions?* Take at least a minute or two to pause, and stay alert to any answers.

Ask the angel realm the following: *Dear angels, Does [name] regret hurting me?* Take at least a minute or two to pause, and stay alert to any answers.

Ask the angel realm the following: *Dear angels, Would [name] take back their hurtful actions if they could?* Take at least a minute or two to pause, and stay alert to any answers.

Ask the angel realm the following: *Dear angels, why is [name] in my life?* Take at least a minute or two to pause, and stay alert to any answers.

Ask the angel realm the following: *Dear angels, is it possible that I can forgive [name], yet their role in my life has come to an end and we should part?* Take at least a minute or two to pause, and stay alert to any answers.

Ask the angel realm the following: *Dear angels, would [name] and I benefit by being in each other's lives for years to come?* Take at least a minute or two to pause, and stay alert to any answers.

Ask the angel realm the following: *Dear angels, is there a wound or trauma or mental/emotional condition [name] experienced/experiences that triggered them to hurt me?* Take at least a minute or two to pause, and stay alert to any answers.

Ask the angel realm the following: *Dear angels, what lessons have I learned from this wound, and/or what blessings in disguise have come from it?* Take at least a minute or two to pause, and stay alert to any answers.

Now picture the person who hurt you…as a child. If you know what they looked like as a child, picture them that way now in your mind's eye. If you didn't know them as a child or never saw a picture of them from when they were young, imagine what they looked like as a child. See them playing, or being cuddled by one of their parents. See how young they are. How innocent. How trusting. How happy. Recognize that there was once a time in this person's life when they had, hopefully, not yet been knocked around by the world. Not been lied to or hurt or abused. This is how the angels see them. That innocent, loving child is still inside the person who hurt you, even if this inner child is buried very deep down. Connecting with the inner child of the person who hurt you might help you forgive them.

If forgiveness still feels elusive with this person even after you have completed this exercise, don't feel guilty and don't blame yourself. Forgiveness can be very challenging. And the angels tell me that forgiveness does not always happen on this side of the veil—sometimes true forgiveness comes in heaven. The angels were with you during this exercise, and you did everything right. You can try this exercise again in a week or so, focusing on this same person. Or instead of forgiveness, perhaps you need to work on moving on from this wound and possibly even this person. Keep working on expressing your emotions, and nurturing yourself as you do so. Talk to supportive loved ones you trust, and consider seeing a professional therapist too. The angels love and support you, always, whether you are able to forgive or not.

Disappointment Can Be a Sign of Something Better on Its Way

Your guardian angels know you are disappointed when a major opportunity or job or person or adventure doesn't work out the way you planned. Your guardian angels want to remind you that no experience is ever wasted. You have learned and gained much from this situation, even if you don't realize it yet. And those lessons will prepare you for other opportunities and jobs and people and adventures that are more suited to you.

There are treasures awaiting you, many of which were set in motion with the help of your guardian angels before you were born. These divinely orchestrated opportunities and jobs and people and adventures will shine like jewels to you, and will seem as if they were forged in the womb of the universe for you and you alone. That is because they were made for you and you alone. But if the experience you just went through hadn't ended, it would have kept you from those treasures Spirit has set aside just for you. Try not to blame yourself. Yes, you may have made a few mistakes, but some things were simply not meant to be. Let that knowledge bring you peace.

While you are hurting over the wound of a major disappointment, be gentle with yourself. It's not important that you understand exactly why things happened the way they did right now. (I didn't realize a job I desperately wanted and was denied was wrong for me until something even better came along six months later. And I didn't realize a relationship I was in that ended was wrong for me until I met my husband a year later.) It is only necessary for you to have faith that you are still on the right path, and that your guardian angels are by your side every moment, loyally standing a 24-hour guard over your existence. Nothing that happens to you escapes their notice. Your guardian angels are always working behind the scenes to bring you closer to your dreams, and to those treasures that were claimed as yours before you were even born.

Angel Affirmation: This disappointment is not the end, and a new beginning custom-made for me is right around the corner.

Changes Big and Small

Change is a reality of life your guardian angels want you to get more comfortable with, because change is the first ingredient in any miracle. Because the angels want you to become a master alchemist, one who can transform the ordinary into the extraordinary, it is essential that you find a way to navigate through changes big and small so that your natural fears of change don't stop you from experiencing all the glittering, gold-dust magic life has to offer.

Ultimately your sense of safety and security should come from your connection to Spirit and the angel realm. All the other details of your life could change in an instant: your friends, your family, your job, your home, your health, your financial situation. The constant is and always will be Spirit, its love for you, and the angels that Spirit sends to watch over you closely every day. The benevolent constancy of Spirit, and the affection and protection of your guardian angels, will never change. Let that unshakable foundation be what grounds you when the future is uncertain, when events leave you blindsided. Let it be what comforts and nurtures you when changes make you feel vulnerable and frightened. Let it be a promise, let it be hope, and let it be the certainty of a safe landing when the topsy-turvy nature of life makes you feel like you're in a free fall.

But the angels want you to let this foundation of faith be even more. Your guardian angels want you to use your faith to take more risks, to take advantage of new opportunities presented to you. The angels want the assurance of their love and guidance and protection to allow you to proactively make more changes in your life, big and small. Changes that challenge you. Changes that nurture you. Changes that fulfill you. Changes that offer you a different perspective. Changes that bring you more joy. Changes that set you free. Changes that make life feel like an adventure. Changes that help you grow and learn, even if they don't work out quite the way you planned. Changes that help you help yourself, and changes that enable you to help others. Changes that might feel a little scary, but exciting!

Call on the angels for support when life throws you a cosmic curveball, and for courage to make the changes your heart yearns for.

Angel Prayer: Angels, let me know you are walking beside me through changes both big and small, and help me find the resolve to initiate those changes that will bless my life and expand my world.

Concentrate on the Little Things

When the big things aren't going your way, concentrate on the little things. Angels love life's details: lavender eye pillows, essential oil perfume, a framed print from your favorite artist, a hot cup of peppermint tea, soft sheets, a new hairstyle, laughing with a cherished friend, snuggling with a pet or a loved one, a good book. Angels appreciate life's details because to angels, every inch of the human journey is precious and magical. Not just the big stuff, but the little stuff too.

Angels also know that the big things—building a career, working on a relationship, starting a family, saving money, earning a degree—can be challenging. Big projects can take a long time to pull off. Big projects are roller coasters of wins and losses, peaks and valleys. And there is only so much control we have over the big things in life. Some of these outcomes are in the hands of Spirit, or are at the mercy of people and factors we can't do much about, like the will of others, the state of the economy, etc. When we get too caught up in our big projects and schemes, or if we're frustrated that the big things don't seem to be going our way, stepping back and turning our attention to the little things can be very calming and healing. Just like concentrating on angels is calming and healing, concentrating on the little things is calming and healing.

The details in life are the best way to nurture yourself, period. Think about the nurturing you get from your angels. Sometimes an angel will save your life, get you a job, or help you find a mate. But your need for this kind of dramatic angelic assistance only happens occasionally. More often angels are interacting with you in your everyday life in much less sensational ways—in the details. Angels whisper words of reassurance in your ear. Offer insightful ideas about a work project that just pop into your head. Help you find the words to comfort a friend. Send your favorite song to you on the radio or in a store. When you're burnt out from working on the big stuff in life, or disappointed because a long-held dream isn't turning out the way you want, or you've just got so many big things in transition in your life that it's become incredibly stressful, you need to nurture yourself. This is when the little things become like Band-Aids for your soul, dabs of divine salve.

Concentrating on the little things is more manageable and gives us back a sense of control. Little things give us a break from the headache of big projects. Little things allow us to lavish ourselves with pleasure and comfort, which gives us back our sense of gratitude. If you've been throwing your hands up in the air over a big project, or tossing and turning at night worrying about your future, treat yourself to a latte. Schedule a massage. Go to the store and get the ingredients for your favorite dinner. Put a little bit of money aside every week in a jar. Take a twenty-minute walk in nature. Watch a favorite funny movie. Clean out a closet. Make a phone call you've been putting off. Research a new hobby. Start a journal. Schedule an appointment with a healthcare provider to have your vitamin, mineral, and hormone levels checked. Take a cooking class. Organize a photo album. Clean your desk. Buy some comfy new socks. Pick one or two pieces in your wardrobe that have been bugging you and update them. Get a free makeover at the makeup counter. Take yourself out to breakfast and sit and linger at the table over the Sunday paper and a cup of coffee. Get dessert. Paint your nails. Sit down with a child or mentee and share with them one of your greatest life lessons. Teach a dog a trick. Plan a close-to-home, cheap weekend getaway with your partner or a friend. Give someone flowers. Give yourself flowers! Give someone a card and inside write down everything you love about them. Watch the sunset. Start a daily fifteen-minute meditation practice. Take a yoga class. Book an Angel Reading with me. Whatever you do, do something little. Do a *bunch* of little things.

Thinking about the big stuff too much can make life feel heavy. Spending time on the details brings a sense of lightness back, like floating through life on angels' wings. The angels want you to remember that there is nothing insignificant about this earthly journey you're on. Spirit is in every detail, and when you concentrate on those details they illuminate your life as much or even more than all those big, bright stars you've been chasing.

Angel Affirmation: I pay close attention to the little things, for the magic and wonder of the universe is revealed to me in the tiniest details of daily life.

ANGEL EXERCISE:
DEDICATE YOUR DAY TO SOMEONE WHO HAS PASSED ON

This angel exercise is intended to ground you in the everyday pleasures of being alive. The angel realm wants you to be more present in your life, to recognize and savor every detail. Often your guardian angels will send you signs and messages meant to wake you up to the joy and meaning in the present moment, like playing your favorite song on the radio, orchestrating an afternoon off when you are overworked, or encouraging a child or pet in your life to give you an unexpected hug or kiss. Likewise, the angels will help you make the following exercise special and memorable.

First, pick someone who has passed on to dedicate your day to. I find this exercise most powerful when I dedicate my day to someone who has passed away young, whether they passed as a child or an adult in their prime. Dedicating your day to these folks reminds you how grateful you are to simply be alive. It can also be inspiring to pick someone who had a real passion for life and found joy easily. You can pick someone you knew, like a close friend or family member, or someone you heard about in the news who touched your heart. Another benefit of this exercise is it can make you feel closer to a deceased loved one, if that is whom you choose to dedicate your day to.

Next, start the day by formally dedicating it to the person who passed on. This should be done with some degree of sacredness and ritual, although the dedication doesn't have to be lengthy or involved. A simple prayer, or a note written down in your journal, will suffice. This makes an impression not only on you but gets the attention of your dedicatee in the Spirit world. (Don't worry, though, angels are expert messengers and will make sure your dedicatee knows they are being honored by you that day!) Include the angel realm in this dedication, asking that your guardian angels help you make this day extra special by sending you surprise blessings and experiences that will delight and inspire both you and the person you are dedicating your day to on the other side. (This really works! Be certain to note these angel gifts at the end of the day in your journal.)

Now, from the moment you step outside your door in the morning or start moving through your day in your home, imagine everything you do from the perspective of the person who has passed on, who would probably be thrilled and excited to have one more day on earth even though they are happy and at peace in heaven. Ordinary activities like eating a bowl of oatmeal with honey take on a sensual decadence. And even routine chores like showering or cleaning the kitchen start to illicit a feeling of gratitude. A hug from a coworker or loved one, a smile from a stranger, a puppy jumping on your leg can suddenly seem like mini miracles.

If you are dedicating your day to a child who has passed on, see the world through the wonder and curiosity and delight of a child's eyes. If you dedicate your day to a relative or friend who has passed, perform some of the activities you know they would enjoy so you feel closer to your departed loved one.

And here's the best part: As you go about your day, make sure to imagine how much the person you dedicated your day to would enjoy these moments. Because…guess what? They are enjoying them! They're watching your day unfold, right along with you, from heaven.

When You're Afraid, Angels Are Closer than Ever

It is tempting to think that Spirit has abandoned us when our lives turn upside down, but the truth is that when you are afraid, your angels are closer to you than ever. You may not be able to see them, but angels are all around you when you are going through times of crisis and challenge. When the future seems uncertain and the present feels unstable, knowing that angels are near can keep you calm. And when you can get a grip on your fear, when you feel grounded and secure, you will make better decisions because you will no longer be making decisions from a place of terror and desperation, but from the knowledge that you are supported by Spirit. The angels are showing me that when you are in crisis and overwhelmed by fear, it's like an alarm is sounded at a fire station. Your own angels jump into action: sliding down poles, gathering hoses, and racing to where you are so they can help put out the inferno.

I first experienced how angels can calm intense fear, and how they are more present than ever during times of crisis, thirteen years ago when my health started to fail. It seemed like one thing after another: stomach problems, hormone imbalances, vitamin and mineral deficiencies, low thyroid, heavy-metal toxicity. I was able to keep working and lead a somewhat normal life, but there were a couple of particularly low points, and a few healing crises. Twice I experienced bottoms where I doubted if I could go on, and during both of these periods I felt absolute terror, on a level I have never encountered before or since. It felt actually terrifying and very unsafe to be in my own body.

The first time I doubted if I could go on living with my condition was around the time I fell ill, and the experience helped solidify my faith—I finally had to simply look up at the sky and say, "Help!" I began praying and journaling to Spirit in a way that I hadn't since I was a teenager. The connection I made to Spirit and the angels, and the signs and guidance I received from them, was what gave me the courage to walk through that specific crisis with my body in a way that was—most of the time—calm and confident. Once I felt Spirit's presence so strongly, it was hard for me to go into the fear of my illness. It was hard to feel anything but safe, no matter the current circumstances of my health. I learned quickly that Spirit was, in my time of need, closer to me than ever, and the guidance Spirit gave me was clearer than ever. This is something phenomenal about crisis: You will start to receive guidance from your angels that is so obvious, so dramatic, so loud, that you'll almost want to look up and say, "I get it! I hear you!" The reason you don't have to let fear overwhelm you in a crisis is because Spirit ramps up its care and attention toward you during these moments.

My second major crossroads in my healing journey (more than ten years ago) was different, mainly because I was already grounded in my faith. Yes, I was still terrified—but only initially. It didn't take long for me to remember the lesson my illness had already taught me—Spirit and the angels were closer than ever. Naturally I had days where I felt scared, cried, or became depressed. Days where I was angry at Spirit and questioned why this was happening to me. But much more often I was able to look at the experience almost as a treasure hunt or game, wondering what new opportunity to heal or learn Spirit would send me that day. Would one of my doctors have a new suggestion about a supplement I could try or a test we could run? Would a friend recommend a book about diet or meditation or self-care? Would I overhear a conversation at my local food co-op that might have some special meaning for me? Would Spirit speak to me through the advice of a loved one? How would I feel Spirit with me when I walked in nature—in the reflection of the moon? In the sound of the wind through the trees? In the face of a child passing by? Just like my last major crisis with my health, I felt the presence of Spirit more strongly than ever. Synchronicities and guidance came down the wire constantly. It didn't take long for me to start trusting that Spirit would send me everything I needed to get through this phase of my life. When fear flared up, my relationship with Spirit helped extinguish the flames relatively quickly.

During both of these health crises, I made some bad choices, cost myself some time, cost myself some money, made things way more difficult than they had to be, didn't nurture myself enough, alienated people, occasionally wallowed in self-pity. In short, it was no picnic! But without my faith that Spirit was right beside me on my journey, I wouldn't have just made mistakes. The fear of my situation would have crippled me. Without a trust in Spirit, I don't know if I ever would have healed. If I had, it would have taken me so much longer and been so much harder. That's because with the reassurance of Spirit's presence keeping my fear in check, I was freed up to pay attention to and act on all the guidance I was being given about how to heal and manage my condition.

I'm sharing this personal story because I think it illustrates the benefits of leaning on your angels in times of fear. And by telling you this story I'm letting you know that, like everyone, I have been in the trenches. When I say that staying close to your angels, reminding yourself of their presence, and watching out for their guidance will help you keep fear in check—and even help you move more quickly and easily through a crisis—I am saying this from firsthand experience.

With the help of many people I did eventually heal most of the conditions I suffered from, and have felt absolutely fantastic and full of energy for the past five years. I still manage my testy tummy, get my hormones and thyroid checked regularly, and stay on a strict regime of supplements and a special diet. My healing journey started fifteen years ago, and it continues today. Whenever I feel fear overwhelm me, I think of my angels.

The angels are showing me an image of glowing white shields. The angels are telling me that during times of fear and crisis they surround you like shields, protecting you, and allowing you, a soulful warrior, to safely forge ahead.

Angel Affirmation: Spirit does not abandon me during crisis. When I am scared, my angels are closer than ever. I watch for their guidance and comfort.

11

———————●———————

Living as a Human Angel

Readers like you who are naturally attracted to celestial angels are yourselves human angels. You probably like hearing about your guardian angels and take great comfort in knowing they are near, because you share many character traits with them: You have an open heart, you are very compassionate, you feel a natural inclination toward underdogs or those who are marginalized by society, you have a hard time turning away from people in desperate states of neediness, you find it difficult to block out or ignore pain on the news or in faraway lands, you can sense and feel other people's emotions—especially those people you care about deeply—as if their emotions were your own, you are most alive and satisfied when you are being of service to others.

Angels don't just fly around in heaven—there are plenty of them walking around on earth. If you picked up this book, and feel like the pages were written just for you, you are indeed one of these human angels, and you have a very special bond with the heavenly angel realm.

Self-Care for Human Angels

Your guardian angels don't have to tell you to take good care of your friends and family, to champion the downtrodden, to create a life of meaning. These are already your instincts, just as they are the instincts of celestial angels. Taking care of yourself, and putting your needs first, however, are probably either lessons you haven't learned, or struggle to consistently implement in your day-to-day life.

Many of you human angels have gravitated toward healing, nurturing professions. You might be a teacher, healthcare professional, mother, father, social worker, artist, chef, or activist. Whatever role you are playing in your professional or personal life—friend or spouse, waitress or real estate broker—you take on that role as sacred, just as your guardian angels consider their responsibilities sacred duties. You probably find yourself going out of your way to give emotional and professional support to your clients, coworkers, and loved ones—often acting as a guardian angel to them. On the surface there is nothing wrong with that. As a human angel it is what you were born to do, to go the extra mile to serve others, and it is how you mine the most fulfillment from your days.

But there is a dark side to your human angel disposition. While your life can have incredible emotional depth, purpose, and passion, you are also more susceptible to burnout, exhaustion, and resentment. Your counterparts in heaven, your winged guardian angels, have an important message for you. A message that might seem counterintuitive to human angels, but one that is vital not only to your own emotional and physical health, but vital to your mission of service here on the planet. This message from your guardian angels is: TAKING GOOD CARE OF YOURSELF IS THE MOST SELFLESS ACT YOU CAN PERFORM. The heavenly angels guided me to write that sentence in all caps not just once, but twice: TAKING GOOD CARE OF YOURSELF IS THE MOST SELFLESS ACT YOU CAN PERFORM.

When you make self-care the cornerstone of your life, you are able to walk through the world as your best self: you will have more energy, you will be more emotionally grounded, you will be in better physical health, you will have a calmer, clearer mind. And here's the part that will most appeal to human angels: *Not only will you feel better when you take exceptional care of yourself, you will also be able to give more to others.*

Being of service to others, usually to those who need it most, is of paramount importance to human angels. It's what you were brought here to do. It satiates your soul, and makes you feel close to Spirit, like nothing else. But to truly realize your destiny as a human angel, you must grasp and embrace the ironic truth that putting yourself first is the best way for you to help others.

Do you have a hard time asking for help? Do you often not realize you are exhausted or burnt out until the situation has reached crisis level and you find yourself exploding or having a mini breakdown? When loved ones ask for your help, do you rush to their aid immediately and without question? Do you commit to things quickly without thinking the situation through, considering how much will be expected of you or how it fits into your schedule? Do you sometimes find yourself resentful of how much you give to others? Are you often overbooked or overscheduled? Do you feel like many of your important relationships are unequal or one-sided? Are you known as the emotional rock of your family or circle of friends? Are you known as one of the most competent and dependable people in the office? Do others tell you their troubles and open up to you in intimate ways even when you don't know them well? Do people in your life express shock or act rebellious when you discuss your needs or dreams? Do you tend to put up with extremely demanding or intolerable situations at home or at work longer than your friends or family would? Are you known as the workhorse at the office or at home?

If you answered yes to even a few of these questions (and I'm guessing many of you answered yes to all of them), put this book down right now and give yourself a good, long hug. Maybe you also need to have a good cry—followed by a good laugh!

Now come back to me for a moment, because there's another crucial message your guardian angels have for you, human angel: There's someone in your life who desperately needs your love and kindness and attention. Someone whom you have left out in the cold and abandoned on too many occasions. That person is you, sweetheart. You've been so busy trying to save your family, save your friends, save your workplace, save the world, that somewhere in there you forgot to save yourself. There's a reason flight attendants always remind passengers to put a mask on themselves before assisting a child.

Maybe what I'm saying doesn't *completely* resonate with you. Maybe you're thinking, "Tanya, I know this stuff. I know I need to make myself a priority. I know I have to take better care of me. I know I have to assert myself." Maybe this *is* stuff you are already aware of, already working on. If so, I applaud you. The angels applaud you! They are even putting two fingers between their teeth and whistling right now. One of them just held up a big foam finger that says "No. 1" on it. (I'm serious!)

But here's something to remember: Whether this angel message on self-care is coming as a total revelation or simply a welcome reminder, you probably don't know that as a human angel, you will *always* be more susceptible to putting yourself last than other people, people who are great people but are not human angels. Human angels actually need to go *out of their way* to take good care of themselves, because your natural inclination will always be to take care of others first. *You need to take on your own self-care with the same sense of sacred duty that you take on the needs of others.*

So, what are some of the practical ways your guardian angels want you to take better care of yourself? Get more sleep and get more rest—by that I mean don't do so much (human angels have an inborn tendency to be hyper "productive" in all aspects of their life). Try to play more and work less (you work so hard you can afford to slack off and do something silly—you'll still be one of the hardest-working people you know). Eat healthy, high-quality, organic food. Make beauty a central part of your life: with your hair and makeup, with your clothes, in your home, at your office, by spending time in nature. Start getting in touch with your own needs and desires, instead of spending your days constantly tracking the emotional and physical needs of your friends, family, clients, and coworkers. Start getting comfortable with asking for help and delegating, and recognizing this as a sign of strength and not of weakness. See others as capable, instead of feeling like you are the only one who can finish a task or do it "right." Start training the people around you to see you as someone with needs and boundaries, because you have probably trained them to see you as an uber-competent superwoman who gives and gives and never needs to stop and fill up her own reserves. The angels are guiding me to add that sometimes this is a very important lesson for spouses and children in your home. Angels are telling me kids are never too young to learn that adults in their life have needs too.

You don't just have one guardian angel, you have a team of angels supporting you. That's because heavenly angels know that caring for others is an enormous job. They would never try to do it alone, and neither should you. Angels love to play and celebrate and rest. They love to learn and better themselves. They love to stop and pray and feel the reverence of Spirit. They love to smell the roses. They love the good life. They love to be pampered. They want the same for human angels.

Change doesn't happen overnight, so be gentle with yourself (and with the people in your life who will have to see you with new eyes) as you work toward making your own self-care more of a priority. You may need the help of a professional, like a therapist or life coach.

Angel Prayer: Guardian angels, mentor me in the art of being an effective human angel. Show me how to take excellent care of myself so that I have more to give others.

Angel Diet/Third-Eye Eating

Would you ever guess that you can create more intimacy with your angels through your diet? I call it the Angel Diet, although I have also referred to it as Third-Eye Eating. The rules of this diet are simple and easy to follow. This diet is healthy and may cause you to lose weight, but I am outlining it here because this diet will increase your psychic ability, your connection to Spirit, and your communication with your angels. Remember, always speak to a doctor, nutritionist, or other trusted health-care provider before making changes to your normal diet.

Angels are sweet, and so are the people who love them—but sugar is too sweet. Sugar can cause your energy to spike and crash. Wildly fluctuating energy is far from ideal when you're trying to stay in close contact with the angel realm. In fact, you want to be open and ready for angelic communication at any time, and for this you need to have even, steady, dependable energy. (Protein is excellent for providing you with the kind of consistent energy

I'm talking about.) Angelic communication can come when you least expect it, often appearing out of the blue, and you don't want to miss these precious messages from your angels because you are lying on the couch strung out on a bag of candy! We all need our treats, and everything in moderation, but it might surprise you to realize how much sugar is added into food that doesn't taste sweet at all. Read labels, and investigate Stevia as a healthier alternative to sugar. Once you cut back on the amount of sugar you consume, your taste buds will adjust, and suddenly a spoonful of unsweetened almond butter will taste like a treat.

Angels are renown for being alert, and admired for their split-second timing. Angels get their quick reactions and intense presence from Spirit, not from caffeine. Abusing caffeine does a number on your human nervous system, which is much more delicate than most people realize. Your nervous system is key when engaged in psychic work and interacting with angels. Humans use their nervous systems to sense angels, to pick up on the subtle energetic shifts that accompany Spirit. When our nervous systems are overloaded with caffeine, this very fine, precise instrument called the human nervous system is thrown into overdrive and incapable of registering something as intricate and sophisticated as Spirit. Some people might be able to handle small amounts of caffeine, and even find it beneficial. But a bottomless cup of strong coffee will leave no room for the subtler influence of Spirit in your palate.

Angels know that everything in our human world comes from the earth, so when angels hear humans talk about natural and organic food…well, the angels can't help but giggle. Yet the angels aren't laughing for long. Angels take the care and protection of the earth very seriously, and feel that it is our job as humans to guard over this paradise we've been blessed with. Angels want us to think of ourselves as custodians of this planet. And harsh, dangerous chemicals and genetically modified food are not the hallmarks of good custodianship. The angels want you to be healthy, and to live a long, productive life. The use of toxic chemicals in your food puts all that the angels want for you at risk. It also puts our planet at risk, as well as every other living creature on it. Organic food has gotten more affordable and plentiful in recent years, and is an enlightened investment in the earth and your family's health. The angels want to see you living up to your destiny, and part of that human destiny for each of us is to be good stewards of paradise. Living as closely aligned as you can to the great destiny intended for you will bring you closer to your angels, guaranteed.

Angels have a very tender spot for animals of all kinds, including farm animals. Whether you eat meat and animal products or not is an individual choice. However, buying food from animals that have been humanely treated should not be a choice, it should be the standard. These products should come from animals who do not live in cages but roam free; animals that are provided with quality food; animals who are not injected with hormones and large amounts of antibiotics. Consuming the flesh of another living thing is a sacred act. It should be done with reverence and mercy. When you take another animal inside your stomach it becomes part of you. This happens temporarily on a physical level, and is one more reason to make sure the animals you take products from are treated and fed well. The animals you eat become part of you on a spiritual and energetic level too. This is why saying a simple grace at mealtime, where you thank any animals that provided you with any part of your meal and set an intention to use their energy to do good in the world, can be a very powerful practice. "Thank you for the fish that gave its life so that I may have life" is a good starting point.

If you do eat meat, consider participating in Paul McCartney's Meat Free Monday campaign. If everyone picked one day a week to abstain from eating meat, it would have an enormous, positive impact on the environment. The angels are asking me to tell you that if you and your family like this experiment, expand it to other days of the week too.

Cats and dogs are not the only animals who need the care and protection of humans. Showing compassion for all animals will give you something in common with the angels, and make you more in tune with your winged friends.

Angels believe in the benefits of having a good time, but angels would never be happy to see you abusing alcohol. My guardian angels are telling me that alcohol was intended to be used only for ceremonial purposes, not to numb ourselves or to relax at the end of a hard day. Whether you choose to abstain from alcohol altogether or only imbibe in moderation, I cannot overstate the benefits of sobriety when honing your psychic abilities. Once that third eye isn't swimming in booze, you won't believe what it's able to see! The moment you stop drinking or decide to keep your drinking to a very moderate level, you will witness your psychic gifts increase significantly (gifts like clairaudience, clairvoyance, and clairsentience that were described in chapter three).

These gifts help you to communicate with the angel realm, and the stronger your psychic abilities the stronger your communication will be with your angels. If you feel that your drinking is out of control, the angels want you to get help. Addiction is nothing to be ashamed of or punish yourself for. And the angels love you unconditionally, whether you seek help or not. But it will be much harder for you to be present and emotionally honest with your angels and yourself when you are constantly under the influence of alcohol.

Angels want you to get all the vitamins and minerals your organs need to properly function. Receiving the right amount of nutrients like potassium, B vitamins, and omega fatty acids will go a long way not only in keeping you healthy but keeping you in closer contact with your angels. The human body is a case or temple that holds a magnificent soul. Therefore the container of this soul should be splendid and running at maximum efficiency. When the body is receiving the proper amounts of vitamins and minerals, it's like plugging in the lights of a Christmas tree. Your body will have an inner and outer glow that matches the radiance of Spirit. Suddenly the machine is getting all it needs, and can operate on the divine level it was intended to. Another way to think of your body is like an antennae for contacting Spirit.

And we want that antennae clean and straight so it can get all the information trying to come down, and send clear information back up! Not only will you be able to connect more easily with Spirit and your angels when you receive all the nutrients your body needs, but you will have the health and energy to do all the good, important work your soul came here to accomplish in the world. You are never closer to the angel realm than when you are being of service, and living your soul purpose. This is because the angels *always* rally around anyone striving to achieve the goals of Spirit in the world.

What else can I say about the Angel Diet? It's not so much divine mystery as it is pure common sense: fresh, filtered water; lots of protein; plenty of vegetables; gorgeous fruit; brown rice. Follow the tenants of this diet and you will not only look and feel healthier, but you will find yourself more sensitive to Spirit and your own psychic gifts. And you know what that means— a closer connection to your angels.

Angel Prayer: Guardian angels, help me take good care of myself and this planet through my diet. Show me where I need to make changes and improvements to my diet.

Let the Angel Realm Help You Be of Service

Your guardian angels want you to experience the thrill of living your passion. The thing that makes you lose track of time, the thing that you would do for free, the thing that is the most sacred part of your identity, this is how you were meant to be of service to the world.

Each human has special gifts, and each of these gifts is needed to heal the earth and its inhabitants and bring this dimension closer to wholeness, closer to heaven. Your guardian angels want to help you find your calling. They will give you clues about your calling so watch out for these clues: intuitive guidance, feelings, and synchronicities about your calling are like divine bread crumbs that lead you home. Your calling is home, because when you are engaged in it you will feel like you are in heaven, with Spirit, your true home.

Your calling may be a role you play in your family, work you do outside the home, or a hobby or volunteer job. Your angels want you to get to know your soul during this life here on earth. Though your soul learns and grows over time it does not fundamentally change. So your calling is a calling your soul has always had, and when you discover that calling it is like meeting an old friend—finally meeting yourself, meeting your soul.

Your calling will involve obstacles and challenges, but you will have such a drive to meet and overcome them that there will be a sweetness even in the struggle. Don't ever let anyone make you feel like your calling isn't important, or is a waste of time. Service is your divine assignment from Spirit, and your guardian angels will work diligently to open the right doors and connect you with the right people so you can succeed.

Being of service to others is the most important part of your earthly mission, for it will also bring you the most joy (another important part of your journey here). Your guardian angels are dedicated to helping you realize this objective of service.

Angel Affirmation: I have a unique divine calling that allows me to be of service to the world. I can always ask my guardian angels to help me understand and make the most of my calling.

Get to Know Your Soul
Through Your Daydreams

Your guardian angels want you to have a sense of the magnificent nature of your soul—of its brilliance and its importance. Your guardian angels are always aware of and in touch with the grandiose nature of your soul. After all they knew you when: before you were born, when you were in heaven with Spirit. They probably knew you in any past lives you've experienced. Your guardian angels know who you are at your core, the essence of you. That eternal part of you that grows and evolves but on some fundamental level does not alter, even over thousands of years and tens of lifetimes. They know your *soul*. And your guardian angels want you to know who your soul truly is as well, because it will help you get in touch with that expansive sense of Spirit—and your purpose in this life.

Every soul has a distinct personality, and one way yours reveals itself to you is through your daydreams. The 1970s rock band Led Zeppelin made a documentary called *The Song Remains the Same* where each member of the group filmed a fantasy sequence. The lead singer arranged footage of himself galloping on a stallion through breathtaking Welsh countryside, finding a sacred sword, and rescuing a princess held hostage in a castle. What does this daydream reveal about the musician's soul? His soul might be a journeyer, an adventurer. Every tour he plays is like a mini quest. Obviously this man is also intensely romantic.

The guitarist shot his sequence at midnight beneath a full moon in the dramatic Scottish Highlands. As he scaled a mountain, a hermit waited at the top, ready to bestow upon the musician profound mystical knowledge. This musician's soul is a scholar, a seeker who is interested in esoteric spiritual subject matter. This person is probably very conscious of how souls grow and evolve and become more and more enlightened over time.

The drummer simply had a film crew take footage of him doing the things he loved best, or his fantasy of the perfect day: dancing around the house with his wife, teaching his son to play the drums, feeding his cows, and driving his favorite motorcycle. This soul is playful, mischievous, and very much enjoys being grounded in its body and this earthly physical plane with all its pleasures.

These musicians were given a rare chance to get to know their souls through an elaborate exploration of their fantasies. But each one of us can do the same by simply letting our imagination run wild. What do you daydream about? How have your daydreams changed over time? Which fantasies are the most consistent? What were some of your earliest daydreams? Your daydreams say a lot about your soul's personality, your purpose here on earth, and where you are in your journey. Daydreams are not an indulgent waste of time. They are incredibly practical and can teach you much about your true divine nature (and possibly offer insight into a past life or future trajectory).

You might be the person who mows the yard, drops the kids off at school, and turns in their taxes on time. But you might also be a healer, a mystic, a performer, a comedian, an explorer, a philosopher, a teacher, a guardian of the earth, a nurturer, an inventor, a craftsman. Wondering what you should do with your career? Pay attention to your daydreams. Looking for a fulfilling hobby? Examine your fantasy life. Want to experience more joy in your day-to-day existence? What do you consistently imagine yourself doing, and how can you incorporate more of these fantasies into your reality?

My most recent recurring daydream? Lady of the Lake, which to me symbolizes someone who is wise, who is a teacher, who works to maintain a close relationship with Spirit. That one started surfacing consistently a few years ago. It tells me a lot about my soul, where I am in my career and spiritual development, and where I'm headed. How can I incorporate more of this daydream into my real life? Writing this book is a good start. Expanding my spiritual practice would be another. Reading books on spirituality helps. Communicating consistently with my angels is essential. Helping people get in touch with their angels, spiritual guidance squad, and departed loved ones in my Angel Readings. And of course I have to wear lots of beautiful, long flowing dresses and sacred jewelry and develop my inner diva, like the celestially named Anjelica Huston in *The Mists of Avalon*. Hey, Lady of the Lake is a rough gig, but some of us have to do it!

Is there a character from myth or history that you feel a special connection to? What is this figure trying to teach you about your soul? How can you incorporate some of what you love about this person into your real life? As always, ask your angels for answers and intuitive guidance when you feel stumped or blocked.

Angel Prayer: Guardian angels, encourage me to indulge my fantasy life, and help me discover ways to incorporate aspects of my daydreams into my current reality.

You Are Worthy

Your guardian angels are powerful, noble, enlightened, incredibly high-vibrational extensions of Spirit...and they chose to spend their time, and dedicate their very existence, to guiding and protecting *you*. That is how important, how *precious*, you are. Each and every living thing on this planet is worthy of infinite love and respect. And each and every person reading these words is a dynamic, wise, talented, *powerful* spiritual being.

Think of your guardian angels as the knights of heaven. Some of the best, bravest, and kindest beings the universe has to offer. And they have pledged their fealty to *you*. That knowledge should inspire you to love yourself, and respect yourself, on a whole new level. And you don't need to do anything to earn that love and respect—from yourself or from your angels. Your worthiness is inherent, woven into the illuminated fabric of your soul by the hand of Spirit itself.

You are worthy no matter your nationality or the color of your skin. You are worthy no matter your religion or cultural background. You are worthy no matter your sexual orientation and whom you love. Whatever your job, whether you are a cashier or a teacher or president of the United States, you are worthy. If you are struggling financially, you are worthy. If your health is challenging, you are worthy. If your career hasn't turned out as you hoped, you are worthy. If you have regrets, you are worthy. If you've hurt yourself and others, you are worthy. You are always worthy, just as you are right now. No matter what you do, say, or think, nothing and no one can ever change the fact that you are living, breathing magnificence.

Once you recognize and step into your own power, your own inherent worthiness as a spiritual being, and realize how much aid Spirit and the angels are prepared to offer you, you can accomplish things beyond your wildest dreams. And that is exactly what you were meant to do. You were meant to heal, to help, to love, to bring this dimension to a whole other level of enlightenment. That is your colossal assignment as a spiritual being, that is what you agreed to before you were born, and that is what you are *more* than capable of pulling off. Yes, actually saving the world is within your power. Once you get that, feel it as truth in your heart and your bones, you can accomplish miracles. People not only step aside to allow you to do your thing, they will offer to help you in extraordinary ways. That's because once you understand just how dynamic you are as an individual, people around you will recognize it too—maybe not consciously, but with even deeper resonance: energetically.

When you enter a room or walk down the street, carry yourself like royalty. There is no person on the planet more deserving, more worthy, than you. You may bow to another out of respect, but realize that it is just as appropriate for them to bow to you, as you might both bow to a fox in the forest, a mountain on the horizon, a star in the sky. We are all spiritual royalty, we are all rock stars of the universe. We each have so much to offer, and in incredibly unique ways.

The angels want you to know that realizing another's power and worth does not negate or "diminish" your own, but enhances it. Have you heard that you are only as good as the company you keep, or the other players on your team? Well, as a citizen of the earth you are surrounded by a phenomenal amount of wisdom, talent, power, and grace. Think of the whole planet as one giant red carpet.

Your guardian angels wish you to recognize not only yourself as a powerful spiritual being, but hope that you will help others recognize this same inherent worthiness in themselves.

Angel Affirmation: I am as unique and magical and precious as a unicorn, existing in a forest of other rare, mystical, priceless creatures.

Trust Your Uniqueness to Banish Jealousy

It's easy to slip into a pattern of jealousy. To wish your life, or some aspect of it, looked more like someone else's. Acknowledging what you admire about someone else's life and letting that inspire you to go out and change your life for the better is one thing. But jealousy doesn't feel inspirational. Jealousy has a stagnant energy that robs you of recognizing and enjoying what is blessed about your life right now. Your guardian angels want to remind you that everyone experiences hardship, pain, and longing. No human is spared these trials during the course of their earthly journey. The angel realm wants to assure you that whomever you are jealous of, that person walks around with heartbreak—and envy for others too. Recognizing this is one way to help ease sensations of jealousy when they arise.

But there's an even better way to stem tendencies toward jealousy, and it will bring you closer to Spirit and your angels— celebrate the uniqueness of your life. There's a lot about your life that is just like everyone else's: You probably have some kind of job or career that provides money to take care of yourself. You have family and friends whom you love dearly. Maybe you have pets who are like family. You have hobbies you are passionate about. You have big dreams and goals that you're working toward. You want to make a difference in the world. You want to feel happy and content. You have some kind of home or other space you can call your own. You believe in angels!

Yet so much about you is unique, including many of the details of your life: the people in your life, your soul purpose, your talents, your growth opportunities, your physical appearance, what you came here to teach others, your quirks, your family. Even your angels are unique! Your guardian angels are assigned to you, and not to anyone else.

Jealousy is about wanting everything to be the same. It's of course natural to want everything to be fair, but wanting your life to look just like another's is a rejection of what makes you and your life unique. And that is a rejection of Spirit, because it is in those places where your life appears most unique, most singular, that Spirit is working through you.

I was raised in a small Texas town by a single mother who died of AIDS when I was seventeen, but basically she exited my life when I was fifteen and I suffered from severe abandonment issues, feeling by the time that I was eighteen (subconsciously) that I was on my own. And in many practical ways I was on my own (although my father paid my tuition and most of my expenses at college, which was an enormous blessing). Those details of my life are fairly unique, especially since this all went down in the late '80s and early '90s, when AIDS was still, relatively, new. Did I look around and get jealous of other kids in my high school class whose lives, at least from the outside, looked a lot more normal? Of course. At the time I was living a nightmare. But was this unique situation I was placed in as a young girl somehow a way Spirit was working through me?

As an adult, I met another woman who'd lost her mother as a teenager. "You have to read the book *Motherless Daughters*," she told me. Author Hope Edelman explains that young women who lose their mothers early often end up taking a lot more risks in life, simply because there is no one standing in the background saying, "Wait, hold on. You're going to move where? You want to be what? That doesn't sound very practical."

My mother's death left me without an anchor in that small Texas town, and led me to Colorado and then to London and eventually to New York City. Her absence meant that no one questioned me when I decided to be a writer. No authority figure was there to suggest it was unrealistic. These decisions—to move around a lot, to end up in New York City, to become a writer—would have been terrible mistakes for most people. But for my unique life purpose, they were perfect. Living in New York City gave me many writing opportunities, and those writing opportunities led me to opportunities to write about angels, which got me closer to Spirit and my own angels, which led me to this book, where I can help you develop a closer relationship with your angels, something I believe is part of my life purpose. Even my mother's disease, one that, at the time, was associated with fear and shame, served me. It made an already very compassionate young woman even more sympathetic to the pain of others because she knew what it was like, at a young age, to be dealt a terrible blow. To watch her mother struggle with the diagnosis and her own mortality at the age of thirty-seven, at a time when having AIDS meant being ostracized from society (my younger brother and I were not allowed to tell anyone my mother had AIDS, and lived in constant terror that someone would find out). If you want to spend your life as a healer, there is nothing more beneficial than really knowing how people in desperate pain and fear feel. But at seventeen it was hard for me to see that perhaps my enforced, unique independence, and my suffering, would actually serve me later in life, and help me serve Spirit in the world.

Of course I am highlighting all the silver linings of this tragedy where my mother lost her life, and I lost my parent. Losing my mother this way, at a young age, naturally had terribly negative effects on my ability to show vulnerability, to ask for and accept help, to know how to take care of myself, to love others, and to love myself. Now in my early forties, despite many years of therapy, reflection, and work on myself, I am still, and always will be, dealing with the ramifications of this early trauma. Looking at some of the blessings that came from my mother's illness and death at first felt counterintuitive and even cruel or disrespectful to my mother's memory and the pain I experienced growing up. But now I find these silver linings an incredible comfort.

Other unique details of my life aren't so dramatic and painful. As a New Yorker I sometimes get jealous of friends and family who live in different parts of the country where they can have large homes and own land. But I'm married to an artist who loves Manhattan. Being married to an artist has made me stronger creatively, and being stuck in Manhattan has helped my career tremendously. So my unique, very tiny New York City apartment might not always be exactly what I crave, but it's serving me and my unique soul purpose, and that is serving Spirit. It helps to remember that when I get jealous of big backyards and remodeled basements!

Angel Prayer: Guardian angels, help me remember that each life is a complex set of circumstances and relationships, and it is in the most unique aspects of my existence that I will meet and serve Spirit.

Have a Noble Heart

It was once thought that nobility had something to do with bloodlines—the family you were born into and their history. Your guardian angels want you to know that nobility has to do entirely with what is in your heart, and the actions you take on its behalf in the world. To have a noble heart means to act with honor. Tales of knights who traveled the countryside doing good deeds might seem old-fashioned, but the world is more in need of do-gooders than ever. As I was preparing to write this section, the angel realm sent me two stories to share with you. Your guardian angels hope these stories will inspire you to walk through the world with a noble heart.

The first incredible story is one you have probably already heard, about a young teacher who risked her life to save her students. This is the kind of story that can't be told and retold enough.[3] I was reminded of this story via a Facebook post that I saw days before I planned to write this section. When I saw this woman's picture staring back at me from my computer screen I got chills, and knew she was the kind of human angel that deserved to be included in this book. Victoria Leigh Soto had just turned twenty-seven, and had only been teaching for

---

3   "Remembering the Passion of a Teacher Who Died Protecting Students," *New York Times*, December 19, 2012; "The Teacher as Hero: Mourning Victoria Soto," *Time*, December 20, 2012; "Teacher from Stratford Shielded Students," Newstimes.com, December 15, 2012; "A Methodical Massacre: Horror and Heroics," *The Hartford Courant*, December 15, 2012

a few years, when a gunman entered Sandy Hook Elementary School. Victoria had time to begin hiding her students (whom she called her "angels") in closets before the gunman reached her classroom. There are different media accounts of what occurred next, and since the only witnesses were small children we will probably never know exactly what happened. But in each version of the story, Victoria emerges as a hero who instinctively risked her life for her students. Some accounts have her acting as a decoy by meeting the gunman in the doorway and trying to convince him that her children were in another part of the building. *All* accounts cite her shielding her students with her own body as soon as the bullets starting flying, and she was key in helping students survive and escape. It is obvious that she was acting on instinct, and her instinct was to protect those children at any cost. As soon as she learned there was a shooter in the building, Victoria went into action to defend her students. This was her only goal, and thanks to this young teacher many of the children under her care survived. Her last act on earth was one of total bravery and selflessness. The teacher who referred to her students as "angels" became their guardian angel that day, a quick-thinking, fiercely protective guardian angel. I sense that Victoria is not the kind of person who would have wanted attention or glory, but the angels are telling me that there is a special place in heaven for people like Victoria, "for heroes" who display great "valor," they say. This is a story I will always carry with me in my own heart, and I hope you will too. Sometimes walking through the world with a noble heart requires a sense of honor that is nothing short of divine.

The second example of nobility that the angels want me to share is not as dramatic. Fortunately most of us are not often, if ever, faced with the kind of decisions Victoria had to make that day. The next story might be more relevant in your own everyday quest to develop, or rather reveal, your noble heart.

The night before I was going to write this section, I was planning out what I would say in my mind. I knew I wanted to write about Ms. Soto, and that the angel realm had made sure I'd seen the Facebook post about her. But I also wanted to give a smaller example of nobility and honor, a more "normal" occurrence. The angel realm must have nudged a family member, who wishes to remain anonymous, to call and share with me the perfect anecdote. (We'll refer to this gentleman here as Hank.)

"I've been running around all day," Hank told me on the phone. "I'm exhausted."

"I thought you had the day off and were going to relax," I said.

"This was a favor for a friend."

"Oh. Did you help them move or something?"

"No, I picked up an extra shift at work," Hank explained. "A coworker there is a single mom, and one of her kids had an accident. She needed four days off to stay home with him, but she only had three vacation days left."

"So did you work the fourth shift for her?"

"Not exactly," Hank said. "She could take the day off without pay, but since she is a single mom she really could not afford to lose the money. I tried to give her one of my vacation days but the company said I couldn't. So I just went to her house and gave her $300."

"Oh, my gosh! That is so nice of you," I said. "What did she say?"

Hank laughed. "She was a little shocked," he replied. "But I insisted that she take it. I told her not to worry: I was going to pick up an extra shift at work to make up for some of the money. So I didn't earn anything today—I just worked a shift for a friend."

"Not only that," I said, "you just helped me write the next section of my angel book!"

A noble heart means treating others the way you would want to be treated. Aren't these words simple and easy to remember? The angels want you to live by them.

Angel Prayer: Guardian angels, show me where I can act with honor, valor, and nobility, and be like the knights of old.

Vulnerability Is Power

I felt guided by the angels to address the subject of vulnerability in this book. As I neared the end of the writing and editing process, I kept asking the angel realm if there was anything else they specifically wanted me to address. The word "vulnerability" was spoken into my mind over and over, even though I hadn't planned on doing an entry on this topic. As usual, I'm committed to letting the angels guide me, and the more I thought about it I realized how important being comfortable with vulnerability is to our earthly journey.

When we think of being vulnerable, we often think of words like "weak" or "exposed." Therefore when we think of someone being in a vulnerable position, we think of them as not having any power. The angels want to point out that the opposite is true: Allowing yourself to feel and show vulnerability—and when appropriate putting yourself in vulnerable situations—is the most powerful way to live your life.

When I think of being vulnerable, I think of showing the world who I really am, and how I really feel. Telling people how much I care for them. Following my dreams even though there is a risk of failure or heartbreak. Loving people even though I can have no way of knowing how our relationship will end. Inviting people to criticize and critique me. Allowing myself to be angry at someone I care about. Genuinely forgiving some-one who's hurt me. Admitting when I'm hurt or disappointed. Admitting when I've let myself down. Admitting when I've hurt someone else. Admitting when I want things to be dif-ferent than the way they are. Speaking my mind even when it makes others uncomfortable. Being fragile. Being delicate.

Being vulnerable always means opening your heart. Your heart is closely linked to the angel realm and Spirit, and that is why vulnerability is one of your greatest strengths.

If you are unwilling to be vulnerable, you may avoid a lot of disappointment and hurt and heartbreak, but you will miss out on a lot of love, victory, excitement, personal growth, opportu-nity, change, and friendship. The angels want you to live at your highest potential. To have the most interesting, full, dynamic version of your life possible. To do that you have to be willing to try new things, to feel unsure, to get let down. You have to be vulnerable—you have to be willing to open your heart.

For people who experienced trauma early as a child or experienced significant trauma as an adult, being vulnerable can be absolutely terrifying. Often these people learned to be tough to survive, to put up protective walls, and they can have difficulty trusting people or the world enough to be vulnerable. But let's face it—being vulnerable can make anyone feel unsafe and scared. The angels want you to protect yourself. They want you to stay safe. But they also want you to live—to practice opening your heart, to practice getting more comfortable with vulnerability. The angels want you to keep in mind that the heart has an infinite capacity to love and an infinite capacity to break—but it also has an infinite capacity to heal.

Ask your guardian angels for help if you find being vulnerable a particularly challenging state. They might send you some opportunities to begin exploring feeling vulnerable in small, manageable ways. And remember that whenever you are feeling vulnerable, your guardian angels are with you, their wings wrapped around you tight.

Angel Prayer: Guardian angels, help me take small, manageable steps toward embracing vulnerability, and remind me of your presence every step along the way.

See Earthly Existence as
the Soul's Great Adventure

Angels want you to look at life as an adventure your soul embarked upon at birth. This life really is a single chapter in a saga-length tale of your soul's existence—a tale the angels are showing me has no end. The angels are giving me an image of a book without a front or back cover (no beginning or conclusion), filled with pages that flip on and on, one turning into the next for infinity.

It's comforting to know that you have a soul that will live on, and possibly have other experiences on earth, but it should also produce a healthy amount of anxiety. This is the only time you get to live this life, and it has an expiration date. Most of us have no clue when that expiration date is—it could come at any moment. So the angels want you to see this life as precious. Another way to think of earthly existence is like the vacation of a lifetime for your soul. If you only had ten days at a vacation destination you'd always dreamed of visiting, you would have a long list of things you wanted to do and see. The same should be true of your time on earth.

Take risks, have fun, go after your dreams. When your soul urges you to move on from a person or experience—heed that advice. Don't let life get stale. Spend your time doing things that are exciting, that challenge you, that teach you and make you grow. Every material possession that you accumulate on earth will be taken from you when you pass away. So don't get too hung up on building an enormous material empire. Of course you want to be comfortable and take care of yourself and your loved ones and give to charity, but passing up opportunities that your heart and soul long to experience simply for stability or more financial gain is probably shortsighted. Earth is not your home. It is only a place you are visiting. Your life's journey should be more about what you do than what you accumulate.

The angel realm is showing me an image of a hero in a fairy tale setting sail on the sea—a hero on a quest—reminding us that this life is like an engaging story our souls have signed up to star in, a story full of twists and turns and victories and defeats. Joseph Campbell wrote about the "hero's journey," a dominant style of narrative that shows up in storytelling across centuries and cultures and mediums. What begins the hero's journey is a call to adventure that eventually lures the hero outside of his normal life or environment. Our life on earth is the call to adventure our souls received in heaven, and accepted. The angels are our mentors or guides—archetypes also present in the typical hero's journey—helping us make the most of this earthly adventure.

Angel Affirmation: The angels encourage me to make my life meaningful, thrilling, and above all a great story.

Pleasure Feeds the Soul

If you randomly opened the book to this page, or if what you read here resonates with you by coming as a relief, making you feel less stressed, giving you a sense of excitement, or even making the hair on your arms stand on end, it's because your guardian angels want you to be more present to life's daily pleasures.

You might be living too much in the past or the future, or so absorbed in a project or goal that whole days, weeks, or even months seem to fly by. Or maybe you're feeling overwhelming pain or anxiety and are holding the present moment at arm's length, and not engaging with the here and now.

When you get out of bed, or walk out of the house each morning, the angels want you to get into the habit of asking yourself, "What can I do today that will bring me pleasure?" There is a common misconception that being close to Spirit involves constant sacrifice or suffering. It is true, sacrifice and suffering have their place in the human journey and can deepen your connection to Spirit. But pleasure, pure bliss, and joy simply for joy's sake are also noble, necessary spiritual experiences.

The angels want you to meditate each morning on what will bring you pleasure today, because pleasure feeds the soul, and the soul needs to be fed daily, or it will wither and fade, just like a malnourished body. Many people think of the soul as a lofty, magnificent spiritual entity, and indeed that is correct. But the soul is also playful. It needs to have fun. Your soul is eternal—it will live on after you are dead, and cannot be killed or destroyed like the human body—yet the soul is still a living thing. The soul still needs daily attention. When we aren't feeding our soul with pleasure we start to sleepwalk through our days. We rush through the hours, or look forward to night when we can go to sleep and put the day behind us. Our soul doesn't disappear, but it shrinks or retracts. We feel less alive, further away from Spirit.

Take special note of the things that bring you pleasure, life's little mercies that are constant, just as the eternal nature of your soul is a constant: phone calls with loved ones who live far away, dates with friends, a strong cup of (decaf!) coffee and a sweet pastry, beautiful clothes on sale, standing in a group of trees, walking hand in hand on a spring day, playing on the ground with an animal, the feel of sunshine on your skin, singing along to your favorite record, laughing at a good story. Your guardian angels want you to understand that these pleasures are not the dessert of your existence, but part of the main course.

Angel Affirmation: Every morning when I wake, one of my first thoughts is, "What can I do today that will bring me pleasure?" And every evening, I make a mental note of the things that consistently bring me joy.

Heaven on Earth

We don't have to wait to experience paradise, but can discover it right here on earth. All we have to do is spend time in the confounding majesty of nature to realize this planet is a legitimate paradise, as beautiful as anything that exists in the universe, including heaven. Many people think of Spirit and the angels as residing only in heaven, but as you've learned by working with the ideas and exercises in this book, Spirit and the angels are all around you.

Although heaven and earth are two distinct places, the angels have explained to me that the division between heaven and earth is largely in our minds. I found that particular piece of information from the angel realm fascinating! We get reminders of how closely linked heaven and earth are when we receive a message or sign from a loved one who has passed on, or when we feel the presence of our guardian angels. Are there differences between heaven and earth? Certainly. Heaven and earth were never meant to be the same. There are experiences and feelings unique to this planet and dimension that your soul came here for. Just as there are experiences and feelings unique to heaven. But the concepts we associate with heaven: love, beauty, miracles, forgiveness, peace, and freedom are also abundant on earth. The phrase heaven on earth really means bringing more of these concepts into our daily lives, and acknowledging the close link and similarities between the two realms.

Your angels want you to know that the concept of heaven on earth is a very important one for every human to explore. Think of it as your top goal in life. The final coordinates on your inner GPS. Like a knight of old, heaven on earth is the noble quest you must either fulfill or die trying to fulfill. When you agreed to come to earth as a soul in a human body, helping to bring this planet closer to heaven on earth was your ultimate mission. There were many experiences and relationships you agreed to be part of, many objectives you agreed to try and reach, but heaven on earth was the end game. Although don't fret; your guardian angels signed on to aid you in your search for heaven on earth, to be with you from birth to death, to put their shoulders to the wheel right alongside you as you live out your unique destiny— the unique ways in which you will bring more compassion and wisdom and fairness and love to this world.

Despite all the pain and horror, the oppression and inequality, the needless suffering and greed that still play out on this planet every second, earth and its inhabitants are getting more enlightened as the years go on. The angels want you to look back on some of humanity's greatest accomplishments—democracy, the end of slavery (in some parts of the world), women's rights, gay rights, equal rights for so-called minorities, better working conditions and health care—and take heart. Look at how far we have come, and let that give you hope regarding how far we have yet to go. How quickly we achieve heaven on earth, and if we achieve it at all, depends on the actions of each individual. No action is too small, and no action is insignificant. Some were born to lead revolutions and ignite progress on a grand scale. But all of us can be more loving, more forgiving. Each of us can do our part to preserve and honor nature. We can create and celebrate beauty. Everyone can stand up for justice, for the underdog. As individuals we create more peace in the world by simply creating more peace in our own lives. We can all achieve more freedom by taking more risks, and by not taking life too seriously. Everyone can practice and promote tolerance. You increase the amount of joy in the world by simply seeking out more joy for yourself, and giving yourself as much pleasure and comfort as possible.

Your guardian angels want you to know that no matter how discouraging circumstances in the world or in your own life may seem, heaven on earth is possible. But only if each person commits to do their part. Your angels can guide you and point you in the direction of heaven on earth. Yet you must take the action steps, must put one foot in front of the other, and move steadily closer to an enlightened planet.

> *Angel Prayer: Dear angels, show me how to make heaven on earth a reality, as well as all the ways my life is already heavenly.*

ANGEL EXERCISE:
RANDOM ACTS OF ANGEL-NESS

Angels are relying on you to help them do Spirit's work in the world. There are countless angels in the heavens, but there are also countless moments on earth that call for love, mercy, and healing. Nurturing, guiding, and protecting the population of planet Earth is a huge job, and the angels need your assistance. You're probably used to asking the angels for help, but now they want to ask you for something: The angels need you to regularly perform Random Acts of Angel-ness.

Whenever you need inspiration for Random Acts of Angel-ness, just open up to this section of the book, or begin a section in your journal called Random Acts of Angel-ness. Record every new idea you get for angelic acts, and record all the angelic acts you perform. You might also write down how the recipient reacted to your angelic act, or how you felt after executing it. Below are a list of possible Random Acts of Angel-ness to get you started. Don't overwhelm yourself: Doing one a day or even one a week is commendable. In time, performing Random Acts of Angel-ness will seem like second nature.

Doing the work of Spirit in the world is a sacred and vital task—and that's exactly why the angels are asking you to help them with it. As a dynamic spiritual being you're more than capable. Be the angel you want to see in the world!

Random Acts of Angel-ness might look like...

1. Complimenting someone on their appearance— not just saying, "You look nice," but remarking on something specific: their hair, their jewelry, their clothes, their smile!

2. Noticing when someone at your workplace or at your school or in your neighborhood looks down. Sometimes simply asking, "How are things going?" and then really stopping to listen can completely change their day.

3. Giving someone you know an extra big smile or enthusiastic hello when you pass them in a hallway. This will make them feel special.

4. Sending a close friend who lives far away a text that says, "Just wanted you to know I was thinking about you today and missing you." It reminds them that there are people all over the world who care about them.

5. Baking or cooking for someone. This could be for the whole office or for a friend or neighbor. Remember, no one has to be in crisis or great need for you to drop off a homemade treat. You don't have to stay and linger when you deliver it either. Just say you had some extra ingredients and thought they'd enjoy a nosh.

6. Offering to pitch in when you see someone is tackling a big job. Whether it's a project at work or chores around the house, offering to handle even the smallest detail can make someone feel less emotionally overwhelmed.

7. Sending a friend a card when they're feeling down. In this day and age a handwritten card is a treasure. Make sure to write on all sides, even the back. You can offer inspiration, tell a funny story from your history together, or give them an update on you. It will remind them that they are not alone, and that will lighten their burden.

8. Opening the door for a stranger—even small gestures like this can re-instill someone's faith in humanity.

9. Holding the elevator for a stranger (again, tiny gestures like this reinforce the idea that we're living in a kind, loving universe).

10. Letting a stranger cut ahead of you in line if they only have a few items or if they seem like they're in a hurry. This reminds them that people aren't always out for number one.

11. Paying the check for a stranger—makes the recipient feel like the universe is a generous, abundant place.

12. Giving a friend a gift for no particular occasion. Remember, you don't have to spend a lot of money.

13. Making a friend a gift for no particular occasion (handmade gifts are always appreciated).

14. Making a loved one a photo album.

15. Sending a friend a note telling them all the things you love and admire most about them (like their smile, their compassion, their talent, or times when their actions have inspired you).

16. Sending someone a thank-you note. Real thank-you notes, whether over e-mail or in letter form, are a dying art.

17. Sending someone a thank-you note for making a big difference in your life. Maybe you couldn't imagine life without a healthcare provider or mentor—write them a note and tell them so (there is something important about seeing it written down in black and white, and if you do this in a card they can keep it forever).

18. Making an effort to spend time with someone who appears lonely.

19. Making an effort to befriend someone who is new to your work or school or community (invite them out to lunch or coffee or stop and chat when you pass them in the hall or street).

20. Finding a way to give back to your community. This can be through a financial donation or a donation of your time.

21. Getting a ten-dollar bill, breaking it into ones, and spreading them around throughout the day to people. (I learned this one from the late, great inspirational author Wayne Dyer—man, will it make your day.)

22. Doing a chore or work project that normally falls to someone else. Don't even tell them you're doing it until it's completed!

23. Making a special dinner for your partner, kids, roommate, friend, or neighbor. When they walk in the door have everything ready, including candles or flowers, and yell, "Surprise!"

24. Smiling and offering a sincere thank you to cashiers or anyone else providing you with a service, especially if they seem like they're having a bad day.

25. Offering to pray for someone. If a loved one has strong faith, they'll be thrilled with an e-mail out of the blue asking, "May I pray for you about something?"

26. Praying for someone every night for a week if they have a great need (examples: illness, financial crisis, etc.).

27. Praying for a stranger.

28. Telling family and friends that you love them often.

29. Offering to mentor someone.

30. When you can afford to, paying someone what you think they are worth, which is usually more than what they will ask for.

31. If someone does a good job, giving them a generous tip—no matter their profession (tipping isn't just for folks who work in restaurants).

32. Giving away things you no longer use.

33. When tragedy strikes, getting in the habit of praying for people and places you read about in the news.

34. Picking up trash you encounter in parks and along the beach.

35. Donating time or money to organizations that protect animals.

36. Donating time or money to organizations that protect the environment.

37. Donating time or money to organizations that help the needy.

38. Giving someone the benefit of the doubt.

39. Giving someone a second chance.

40. Throwing someone a party or taking them out to a special dinner to celebrate a milestone in their life or a big accomplishment (sometimes people need a little encouragement to celebrate themselves).

41. Standing up for someone if they are being attacked verbally or their reputation or honor is being called into question.

42. Standing up for what you know in your heart to be right.

Conclusion

As soon as I started communicating with and studying angels, friends and family started coming to me when they had a special request for the angel realm. "My grandmother's in the hospital," a friend told me on the phone. "I need you to pray to the angels for her."

"I've got a big meeting tomorrow at work," another friend e-mailed me recently. "Promise me you will talk to the angels about it. Promise me!"

And now that I am getting a reputation and spreading my wings, so to speak, as an angel author, fans are starting to ask me, "Can you send me an angel?" or "Can you contact the angels for me?"

I love being everyone's go-to angel person, and as many of you already know there is a singular kind of joy derived from praying for someone else. But when folks come to me with requests for the angel realm, I always gently remind them that they can make requests of the angels just as easily as I can. All prayers are heard just as clearly as mine, and all needs are given just as much priority as my own. We each have guardian angels, and we each have access to the angel realm. The only thing we need to do to reach out to our angels is simply talk to them. Say a prayer silently. Ask for help in your journal. Tell your angels your worries and dreams at your angel altar.

The best person to make a request of the angel realm on your behalf is always you. After all, it is your free will that has the power to invite the angels to play an even larger role in your life. And who better to explain the contents of your heart, and advocate for your dreams, than you? (I do offer private Angel Readings that are a powerful compliment to your own direct communication with angels.)

I hope this book makes you feel more comfortable and confident about going directly to your angels for guidance and assistance. You don't have to be an angel expert to access the angel realm. Angels are always listening, always eager to help, and no one has a greater claim on the angel realm than you do. There is no reason to be intimidated by angels—the angels tell me that they are more like us than we think. To the angels all humans are equal, we are all important, we are all deserving of mercy, we are all infinitely lovable, and we are all full of potential.

Let's keep in touch! Sign up for my newsletter or book a private Angel Reading with me at tanyarichardson.com, and follow me on social media at facebook.com/TanyaRichardson-Blessings, @TanyaBlessings on Twitter, and youtube.com/c/TanyaCarrollRichardson for regular updates on the angel realm, new angel exercises, and reminders of the presence of angels in your life.

Angel blessings to you and your loved ones!

All my love,
Tanya

"Were you to realize the forms minute and glorious, which invisibly play their parts in service around you, there could be no monotony—only a divine rapture of gratitude for such ministry." ~*Flower A. Newhouse*

Recommended Reading

Angels in My Hair: The True Story of a Modern-Day Irish Mystic by Lorna Byrne

Archangels and Ascended Masters: A Guide to Working and Healing with Divinities and Deities by Doreen Virtue

The Art of Extreme Self-Care by Cheryl Richardson

Ask Your Guides: Connecting to Your Divine Support System by Sonia Choquette

Heaven on Earth: A Guided Journal for Creating Your Own Divine Paradise by Tanya Carroll Richardson

The Highly Sensitive Person by Dr. Elaine N. Aron

Hiring the Heavens: A Practical Guide to Developing Working Relationships with the Spirits of Creation by Jean Slatter

Transforming Fate Into Destiny: A New Dialogue with Your Soul by Robert Ohotto

You Already Know What to Do: 10 Invitations to the Intuitive Life by Sharon Franquemont

GET MORE AT LLEWELLYN.COM

Visit us online to browse hundreds of our books and decks, plus sign up to receive our e-newsletters and exclusive online offers.

- **Free tarot readings • Spell-a-Day • Moon phases**
- **Recipes, spells, and tips • Blogs • Encyclopedia**
- **Author interviews, articles, and upcoming events**

GET SOCIAL WITH LLEWELLYN

Find us on Facebook

www.Facebook.com/LlewellynBooks

Follow us on

www.Twitter.com/Llewellynbooks

GET BOOKS AT LLEWELLYN

LLEWELLYN ORDERING INFORMATION

Order online: Visit our website at www.llewellyn.com to select your books and place an order on our secure server.

Order by phone:
- Call toll free within the U.S. at 1-877-NEW-WRLD (1-877-639-9753)
- Call toll free within Canada at 1-866-NEW-WRLD (1-866-639-9753)
- We accept VISA, MasterCard, Discover and American Express

Order by mail:
Send the full price of your order (MN residents add 6.875% sales tax) in U.S. funds, plus postage and handling to: Llewellyn Worldwide, 2143 Wooddale Drive, Woodbury, MN 55125-2989

POSTAGE AND HANDLING:

STANDARD: (U.S. & Canada)
(Please allow 12 business days)
$30.00 and under, add $4.00.
$30.01 and over, FREE SHIPPING.

INTERNATIONAL ORDERS:
$16.00 for one book, plus $3.00 for each additional book.

Visit us online for more shipping options.
Prices subject to change.

FREE CATALOG!

To order, call
1-877-NEW-WRLD
ext. 8236
or visit our
website